Reflections of a Tomboy Grandma

Diane Perkins Castro

ISBN-13: 978-0-9986297-0-4 (Paperback Edition)
ISBN-13: 978-0-9986297-1-1 (Ebook Edition)

Library of Congress Control Number: 2017904677

Cover Design by Christine M. Castro

ID Publishing House
IMAGO DEI
Beverly, MA

DEDICATION

Dedicated to all the nameless, faceless people who are
unknown to the world but known and loved by God.
He has not forgotten you; your names are engraved
on the palms of His hands (Isaiah 49:15-16).

FOREWORD

And gladly wolde she lerne, and gladly teche.
—After Geoffrey Chaucer's *The Canterbury Tales*

Who can find a virtuous woman?
    for her price is far above rubies.
She stretcheth out her hand to the poor;
    yea, she reacheth forth her hands to the needy.
Strength and honor are her clothing;
    and she shall rejoice in time to come.
She openeth her mouth with wisdom;
    and in her tongue is the law of kindness.
      —From Proverbs 31 (King James Version)

I first met Diane when a new Anglican church opened its doors near my home in the fall of 2009. She was one of its founding members and one of the first to make me feel welcome in the new church. She has served as a greeter, an usher, a Scripture reader, and an active participant in many areas of church life, from home study groups to kitchen crew.

On the personal level, she has ministered to many people, reaching out to those in physical or emotional distress, taking them into her home in times of trouble, praying for them, and giving practical aid such as meals and transportation.

Diane also taught a small study group in her home. She was always well-prepared, she was highly skilled in presenting the material, and she encouraged all participants to express their thoughts, all while she maintained a friendly environment characterized by mutual respect. (The snacks were good, too!) As a teacher myself, I think she is among the best I have seen at leading a small group. Her ability to explain differing word meanings in the Hebrew and Greek Scriptures is extraordinary, and she communicates her faith in an engaging way. She is committed to maintaining Christian unity and tries to practice the principle "In the essentials unity, in the nonessentials liberty, in all things charity."

In short, she excels in *faith* and *works*.

Over the years I have had opportunity to read some of Diane's writings, and I have encouraged her to publish them so that others might benefit. Through her stories and lessons she shows the immeasurable worth of every person. As a biologist who has taught courses on human life from conception to birth, I have a deep appreciation for the miracle of life and the uniqueness of every human being. I have also been greatly influenced by the experience of teaching special-needs classes; every single life has value. I hope that through the pages of this book you will get to know Diane and explore with her the profound significance of the fact that we are created in the image of God.

John David Koob
April 2017

CONTENTS

INTRODUCTION

As a new Christian in my freshman year at Cornell University, I devoured books about the defense of the faith. I was thrilled to find a philosophical system that made sense of life and answered the big questions: Who am I? Where did I come from? Where am I going? What is the purpose of life? At a campus ministry retreat I met my future husband, Tony, who was getting his masters in astrophysics. Together with other Christians we discussed theological questions, witnessed to the lost, debated with atheists, and made fun of the interfaith center, Anabel Taylor Hall, which we called "Ana-Babel," considering it a tower of confusion. It was a challenging and stimulating environment, with students of every religious and non-religious persuasion, and intellects like Carl Sagan to put our faith to the test. The following year, in order to become further equipped, I transferred to a small Christian college to pursue biblical studies while Tony attended seminary.

But the longer I lived, the *less* sense life made. As our family grew—eventually to include three daughters and three sons—we experienced the trials and sorrows, as well as the joys, of being parents, and I worried about my children's future. It seemed that the world just kept getting worse—whether because I knew more people and so became aware of their afflictions or because I was becoming more sensitive to tragedy all around me or because the media bombarded us with images of horror around the globe or because the world truly, objectively was disintegrating. In any case, the neat and tidy answers that were so satisfying when I was a college freshman didn't work anymore.

We dutifully continued attending church and trying to raise our children in the faith, but often I felt like a failure. I couldn't make my family what I wanted it to be. I couldn't comprehend why God acted the way He did—or more often, why He failed to act the way I thought He should. The joy and hope that supposedly were integral to the Christian life seemed to elude me. I had many questions that were not answered by apologetics or Christian books or sermons. Even the Bible seemed to offer more questions than answers.

Now in my seventh decade, I still get the feeling at times that I am just muddling through life, but I have come to rest in two great declarations about God: that He is good and He is all-powerful. Therefore I can have complete confidence that He is both willing and able to do good and that, despite appearances that often seem to scream the opposite, everything He does has a good and loving purpose. And I have assurance that every single human being on the planet, including me and my loved ones and those I don't know or don't love, is created by God in His image and is cherished by Him and has great worth.

These basic truths guide us in how to live our lives here on earth. The ramifications of them in every area of human thought, actions, and relationships are staggering. This collection of essays is the result of my attempting to understand and implement the principles that should inform the way I think, the way I live, and the way I treat others. My prayer is that these thoughts would stimulate you to take stock of your life and find God's good and loving purposes for you.

Diane Perkins Castro
April 2017

"YOU CREATED MY INMOST BEING"

In October 2015, the *New York Times* ran the story of George Bell, an old man who died alone in his apartment in New York City, unnoticed until the stench of his corpse revealed his passing. Although George Bell died in obscurity, as author N. R. Kleinfield researched his life he found a rich and intriguing history. In Kleinfield's words, "In discovering a death, you find a life story and perhaps meaning."

George Bell's story was just one of many that caught my attention after our pastor, Father Tim Clayton, preached a sermon about "the inestimable worth of every person." The following Sunday, both the choir anthem and the offertory hymn were based on Psalm 139, which tells how God forms us in the womb, knows all our thoughts, and guides all the events of our lives. As I started becoming more intentional about recognizing the value of every single human life, I kept noticing people whose life stories touched me in some way, and I thought about how each one has a unique identity and is known by God and precious to Him.

I heard for the first time the remarkable story of Emma Rowena Gatewood, who in 1955 at the age of 67 hiked the entire 2,168 miles of the Appalachian Trail. She did it again at age 72, and then again in sections at age 75. Another incredible story is that of Minka Disbrow, who at age 16 was assaulted and raped. She became pregnant and gave up the baby girl for adoption, but always longed to know her daughter. God remembered her, heard her prayer, gave her grace through seventy-seven long years of waiting, and granted her request before she died.

I also learned about Martin Pistorius, who at the age of 12 fell into a coma. For nearly ten years it seemed that nobody was home in his body. He later said, "For many years I was like a ghost. It was like I wasn't there. I was invisible." Then a therapist noticed a glimmer in his eye and realized that he was aware of everything going on around him. Through intensive therapy he regained some use of his body and learned to communicate by computer. He earned a degree, got married, and wrote a book about his life, *Ghost Boy: My escape from a life locked inside my body.*

The little daughter of our friends Amy and Erick was born with Down Syndrome. Her mom is chronicling her life as "Evie the Extraordinary," and truly she is an extraordinary little girl, with a bright future. Some other friends have a son with Down Syndrome. He struggles with basic skills, but when he was a teenager they discovered that he had an aptitude for pottery. He now

Evie the Extraordinary

has his own business, Christian Royal Pottery. As Christian's website explains, "A simple beginning has developed into a vocation—one which daily animates Christian's life with purpose, camaraderie, and identity in society." Some of his exquisite pieces hang in our dining room.

A Nightline segment on October 19, 2015, featured Jaxon Buell, a precious little baby who was born with most of his brain missing. Many parents would have chosen to abort a baby with such a condition, knowing that he might not make it to

Jaxon Buell

birth and probably would not live long afterward. But Jaxon's parents loved him even before he was born, even with only part of a brain, and they are "trying to give him the best life possible, knowing it could be a short life." Even in his short time on earth, he has drawn people to Christ. Against all odds, Jaxon has celebrated his second birthday, and his parents know that his little life has a big purpose in God's good plan.

Each of these people, great or small, famous or unknown, has worth and purpose. So do all the people who are nameless and faceless to us, but intimately known by God. How many more George Bells are there in New York and around the world? The story of Grandma Gatewood is a triumphant one, but another AT hiker met a tragic end. Geraldine Largay had hiked almost 1,000 miles of the Appalachian Trail and then she vanished in an isolated area of western Maine. Her remains were discovered more than two years later in the wilderness about two miles from the trail. On the day that her remains were found, search crews found the body of another hiker, Claire Marie Cocuzzo, in the White Mountains of New Hampshire. Both of these women died alone, the story of their last days known only to God.

The haunting images of Alan Kurdi, the little Syrian boy who drowned when the boat in which his family was trying to escape the violence in Syria capsized, tell only one story among millions of refugees. Alan's dad, who lost his wife and both sons when they slipped through his hands in the rough seas, asks, "Is there anyone whose children are not valuable to them?" He is like myriads of parents around the world who only want to provide a safe home for their children. Now, he says, "Everything I was dreaming of is gone. I feel that my life is over."

The plight of the Syrian people is well known, but have you heard of the Rohingya people of Myanmar? They were featured on Nightline on October 21, 2015. For decades the Rohingya Muslims have been the victims of appalling human

Protest against the persecution of Rohingya people in Myanmar
Photo from the BBC

rights abuses. As Matt Smith, founder of the human rights organization Fortify Rights, told ABC News' Bob Woodruff, "It is so bad here that the best option is to face death, torture or abuses at sea or in Thailand just to escape."

We also have countless examples in the Bible of people who had little value in the eyes of the world but were known by God and important to Him. Many were refugees, just like modern-day refugees, fleeing from oppression or famine and seeking a haven for their families. In our women's Bible study we were studying the life of Ruth the Moabitess. Her future in-laws had fled from Bethlehem to Moab to escape a famine. She married one of the sons, but her father-in-law, her husband, and her brother-in-law all died. It seemed that all was lost for Ruth and her mother-in-law, Naomi, but in His providence God took them back to Bethlehem, where Ruth married again and gave birth to a son who would become the grandfather of King David. So a poor foreign girl became God's vessel to carry on the line from Abraham through David to Jesus, the Messiah.

When you hear stories like these, do you think about each person *as a person*? Do you consider the fact that each and every one of these people, like every person who is now or ever has been on this planet, is a human being created by God in His image, intimately known to Him, and dearly beloved by Him? Not just the lovely and loveable people but also the lonely ones like George Bell and the little ones like those lost in the womb and the nameless ones like the refugees and even the bad ones like the persecutors and abusers. If as Christians we want to reflect the character of our heavenly Father, then we need to see people through His eyes and to love not just our near neighbors but also our distant fellow human beings and even our enemies. Or as Mr. Rogers would say,

> As human beings, our job in life is to help people realize how rare and valuable each one of us really is, that each of us has something that no one else has—or ever will have—something inside that is unique to all time.

There are three ways to ultimate success:
The first way is to be kind.
The second way is to be kind.
The third way is to be kind.
—Fred Rogers, adapted from Henry James

FEAR, FAITH, AND FREEFALL

A few years ago my son Alex called me from Florida, where he was going to school, and said, "Hi, Mom, just wanted to let you know that I'm about to jump out of a plane." I said, "You're *what*? And what do you mean you're *about* to? Couldn't you at least wait to tell me until after the fact?" As it turned out, the wind was too high to jump that day and they had to wait until the next day, so I had a full twenty-four hours to worry. But he did it and he loved it and he was fine.

Not long after that, I went down to visit him. A day or two before I went, we were talking on the phone and he asked me what I'd like to do while I was there. I said, "What would you suggest?" He said, "I'd recommend skydiving." Some friends had given me some mad money for my birthday and told me to buy something or do something out of the ordinary. I don't think skydiving was quite what they had in mind, but I figured that it counted as being out of the ordinary, and I said OK.

As it happened, the only day we could do it was the day I arrived. Alex picked me up at the Tallahassee airport and drove me to the municipal airport, and there I watched a video that showed what I was getting into. This was not to be a solo jump, where you get extensive training, learn all the skills involved, and do simulated jumps before leaping out of a plane on your own. It was a tandem jump, where you are harnessed to the instructor.

It occurred to me that walking by faith is a bit like making a tandem parachute jump. There were certain decisions I had to make beforehand—like going to the airport, watching the video (which shows what will happen and tells you all the things that can go wrong), and putting on the harness. But once I was fastened to the instructor, I didn't have to panic about what to do; all I had to do was follow his instructions. The most important choice I made was to allow myself to be harnessed to the instructor, and then he took over. I didn't even have to get up the courage to jump out the door. The instructor counts to three and goes, and you go with him, like it or not. Then I just had to breathe (and in fact, I failed to do that for the first minute, during the freefall). I didn't have to worry about when to open the chute. I didn't have to worry about steering it, to make sure we ended up where we were supposed to and not in the middle of a highway or tangled in power lines or up in a tree. I didn't have to do anything for the landing; he brought us in at an angle so gently that it was like walking—or floating—down a few steps.

In short, a successful jump didn't depend on my courage or my skill or my judgment. I was securely attached to the instructor, and he was in charge. I had to obey him and trust that he knew what he was doing, but he was the one who did it. Similarly, we need to trust Jesus enough to attach ourselves to Him; He is responsible for our safety and well-being.

There's another way that dropping out of the sky from three miles up is similar to walking in faith—it's terrifying and exhilarating at the same time. As we were falling, I yelled, "I can't believe I'm doing this!" You feel the wind rushing past you and watch the ground rushing up toward you, and you wonder what you were thinking when you said you would do it. I imagine the disciples felt the same way when they were sent out by Jesus to heal the sick, or Peter when he was walking on the water. But you also feel alive and aware, and when you catch your breath, you can enjoy the spectacular beauty.

As we were coming down I took a picture that shows just my legs and feet, dangling a couple miles above the earth. My situation *appears* to be very precarious, but in fact, I was very safe. I was in the hands of someone who knew what he was doing. I couldn't see him because he was behind me, but he was in complete control.

If you have never attached yourself to Jesus, let this be the year that you put your trust in Him. If you already know Him, rest in the assurance that He has got your back and will not let you go. If you feel that your life is plummeting out of control or dangling precariously, think of my feet, which are attached to my body, which is attached to the instructor. It might feel scary or dangerous, but you are safe in Jesus' hands. Trust Him, do what He says, savor the ride, and let Him do the maneuvering!

> I am the vine; you are the branches. If you remain in me and I in you, you will bear much fruit; apart from me you can do nothing…. This is to my Father's glory, that you bear much fruit, showing yourselves to be my disciples." (Jn. 15:5, 8)

"I HAVE CALLED YOU BY NAME"

A little boy was looking at a plaque in his church that listed the names of men from the congregation who had been in the military and had given their lives in service to their country. He asked, "Pastor, who are those people?" The old pastor replied solemnly, "Son, those are boys who died in the service." The little boy looked up wide-eyed and asked, "Pastor, did those boys die in the 8:30 service or the 11:00 service?"

All of us want our names to be known and remembered, because it means that our lives have value, that we matter to somebody. We honor people by putting their names on plaques and statues and tombstones and trophies. Having your name immortalized in a hall of fame is a huge honor and must be terribly exciting.

But as thrilling as it is to be in a hall of fame and to have your name known all over the world, it can't begin to compare to being known by God. He knows each of us *by name*. And He came down to earth as a human being so that we could know Him personally. Look what He did for Mary Magdalene. When Jesus died, His followers were devastated and they ran away in fear and discouragement. Not really knowing what to do, Mary went to the tomb and stood there crying (actually, the word means she was wailing with grief). John tells what happened next in chapter 20 of his gospel. This passage contains what I think is one of the single most exciting words in the whole Bible.

> Then Mary turned around and saw Jesus standing there, but she did not realize that it was Jesus.
>
> "Woman," he said, "why are you crying? Who is it you are looking for?"

11

Thinking he was the gardener, she said, "Sir, if you have carried him away, tell me where you have put him, and I will get him."

Jesus said to her, "Mary."

Jesus' utterance of that name, "Mary," thrills me every time I read it. Why? First of all, because it shows that He's *alive*. He had been totally dead for three days, and now He is fully alive. Secondly, it shows that He cares about people personally. He saw Mary's distress and He gently spoke her name. As soon as He said her name, she instantly recognized Him and was filled with joy. Especially significant to women is the fact that Jesus' first appearance after He rose from the dead was to a lone woman, whom He called by name. That one name, four letters, captures a key point of the Bible— that God is alive and that He wants to have a relationship of love and intimacy with us.

Sometimes the people of Israel got to thinking, "God has forgotten us, He doesn't care about us." They were wrong; listen to God's words in Isaiah:

> But now thus says the LORD, he who created you, O Jacob, he who formed you, O Israel: "Fear not, for I have redeemed you; I have called you by name, you are mine" (Is. 43:1).

> Can a mother forget the baby at her breast and have no compassion on the child she has borne? Though she may forget, I will not forget you! See, I have engraved you on the palms of my hands (Is. 49:14–16).

Your name is permanently engraved on His hand. If He even calls every star by name, how much more does He know *your* name!

> Lift up your eyes and look to the heavens: Who created all these? He who brings out the starry host one by one and calls forth each of them by name. Because of his great power and mighty strength, not one of them is missing (Is. 40:26).

He will never forget you. He will never forsake you. You will never go missing. As God says in Jeremiah, "I have loved you with an everlasting love; I have drawn you with unfailing kindness" (31:3).

Let this short prayer from Psalm 17 be your own:

I call on you, O God, for you will answer me.
Give ear to me and hear my prayer.
Show the wonder of your great love.
Hide me in the shadow of your wings.
Keep me as the apple of your eye.

"WHAT IF YOUR BLESSINGS COME THROUGH RAINDROPS?"

On Thursday, June 4, 2015, my brother-in-law Bill slipped into eternity after a valiant battle with leukemia. Five days later, his many friends and family gathered to celebrate his life and to support my little sister Linda, who had been widowed for a second time. Her first husband, Harry, died of cancer at age 33, just after graduating as a physician's assistant, leaving her with a two-year-old son, Josh. Now the unimaginable has happened again.

Why did God take a young man, just as he was poised to serve people with his medical training? Why did God leave a little boy fatherless? Why did He leave Linda to raise Josh alone, and then give her another husband, only to take him too? Why did He let Bill go into remission, only to strike him again? Why did the healing that so many prayed for not come? Why did Bill not even live one more day, until his son Nick graduated from Navy boot camp? Why is Linda left alone, now with both boys grown and gone?

Nick (right) with his brother Mike

We have no answers to these questions, but the song that my niece Kristen sang at the funeral asks some other questions that offer some insight and a ray of hope. "Blessings" by Laura Story poses some "What if" questions that give a glimpse into God's gracious purposes:

What if Your blessings come through raindrops?
What if Your healing comes through tears?
What if a thousand sleepless nights are what it takes
    to know You're near?
What if trials of this life are Your mercies in disguise?

Maybe God gives us gifts through grief, and we have to open our eyes to see and receive them. Bill's obituary listed his many family members and said, "An unexpected gift during Bill's illness was treasured time to build and strengthen these relationships." His death brought together many members of our extended families as well as friends from many walks of life. We're thankful that Bill and Linda were able to take Josh and Nick on a cruise while Bill was in remission, before the boys left the nest. Although Bill didn't get to go to Nick's graduation, we're grateful that he knew that his son had passed all his requirements and was successfully launched. And we will never know in this life how God has been working in the lives of those who were connected to Bill.

My sister Jan has walked this path herself, having lost her fiancé in a car accident three weeks before they were to be married. As Jan said in her meditation at the funeral, Bill was a big, strong guy, but his strength could not defeat death. He faced his illness with courage and determination (and stubbornness!), but those qualities could not conquer death. Neither could all the money poured into his treatment nor all the skill of his medical team nor state-of-the-art technology nor the arsenal of medicines given to him nor the loving and diligent care provided by Linda and countless others. *Nothing* we do can ultimately overcome our greatest enemy, death.

But as Jan explained, there is One who has completely vanquished death. There is a Redeemer who is fully able to rescue us from sin and death. The Old Testament Scripture reading at the funeral was from Job 19:

I know that my Redeemer lives,
and that in the end he will stand on the earth.

And after my skin has been destroyed,
yet in my flesh I will see God;
I myself will see him
with my own eyes—I, and not another.
How my heart yearns within me! (25-27)

The New Testament reading identified the Redeemer: Jesus Christ—the Way, the Truth, and the Life (Jn. 14:6). Although we don't yet see the fullness of it, Jesus secured the victory on the cross and sealed it with His resurrection from the dead. Death could not hold Him in the grave, and neither will it keep its hold on those who look to Him:

"For my Father's will is that everyone who looks to the Son and believes in him shall have eternal life, and *I will raise them up at the last day*" (John 6:40).

By his power God raised the Lord from the dead, and *he will raise us also* (1 Cor. 6:14).

Fight it as we may, none of us can defeat death or avoid going to the grave. But the grave is not the end of the story:

We were therefore buried with him through baptism into death in order that, just as Christ was raised from the dead through the glory of the Father, we too may live a new life (Rom. 6:4).

And what is the point of rising from the dead? To come back to this life as it is would be pretty depressing! Paul says that we are raised so that we may "*live a new life*." Our physical bodies will be transformed and we will be renewed inwardly so that we are the kind of people we ought to be. Brokenness will be healed and relationships will be restored. There will be no more death or mourning or crying or pain.[1]

How can we be sure that all these declarations are not just empty promises or wishful thinking? Jesus put His money where His mouth is by promising to rise from the dead and then pulling it off. If He can triumph over death, He can and will fulfill any promise He makes.

Even in our pain we see hints that something better is to come. Every human being knows that something is desperately wrong with this world and wishes for a better world. That universal longing points not to a wishful fantasy but to a glorious reality—the reality that God will redeem and restore His creation. As Laura Story sings,

> When friends betray us,
> When darkness seems to win,
> We know that pain reminds this heart
> That this is not our home.
>
> What if my greatest disappointments
> Or the aching of this life
> Is the revealing of a greater thirst this world can't
>   satisfy?
> What if trials of this life—
> The rain, the storms, the hardest nights—
> Are your mercies in disguise?

---

[1] See Romans 6:4, Philippians 3:21, 2 Corinthians 4:16, Colossians 1:22, Revelation 22:2; Ephesians 2:14, Revelation 21:4.

A GOOGOLPLEX OF GRACE

Lucy: Schroeder, what do you think the odds are that you and I will get married someday?
Schroeder: Oh, I'd say about googol to one.
Lucy: How much is a googol?
Schroeder: 10,000,000,000,000,000,000,000,000,000,000,000, 000,000,000,000,000,000,000,000,000,000,000,000,000, 000,000,000,000,000,000,000,000,000,000.
Lucy: **Sigh**
—Charles Schulz

Many years ago, while writing features for a children's math book, I learned that the term *googol* had been invented by a nine-year-old boy in 1938. Milton Sirotta was the nephew of Edward Kasner, an American mathematician. Kasner was looking for a name for a very large number—1 followed by one hundred zeroes—and young Milton came up with *googol*. This number is inconceivably huge—10 to the hundredth power, vastly more than the number of atoms in the universe.

When I think of all the sin in our world, its magnitude seems to be like a googol—so immense that it staggers the imagination. Sin has overwhelmed and engulfed our world to an extent that is incomprehensible to the human mind. Thinking of the magnitude of sin and our complete inability to conquer it can lead one to despair.

BUT where sin abounded,
grace did much more abound! (Rom. 5:20)

The magnitude of God's grace is like a *googolplex*—10 to the googol power, the number 1 followed by a googol of zeroes. A googolplex absolutely dwarfs a googol into nothingness, just as God's grace is powerful enough to dwarf sin into nothingness. If you have trouble wrapping your head around a googol, you can't even begin to fathom a googolplex, just as we can't even begin to plumb the depths of the immeasurable grace of God.

Hymnwriters have attempted to express poetically how much greater is grace than sin. The next time you sing one of these hymns, try to imagine how a googol of sin is utterly inundated and overwhelmed by a googolplex of grace.

Marvelous Grace of Our Loving Lord
Marvelous grace of our loving Lord,
Grace that exceeds our sin and our guilt,
Yonder on Calvary's mount out-poured,
There where the blood of the Lamb was spilt.

Grace, grace, God's grace,
Grace that will pardon and cleanse within;
Grace, grace, God's grace,
Grace that is greater than all our sin.
—Julia H. Johnston

This Is My Father's World
This is my Father's world. O let me ne'er forget
That though the wrong seems oft so strong, God is
    the ruler yet.
This is my Father's world: the battle is not done:
Jesus Who died shall be satisfied,
And earth and Heav'n be one.
—Maltbie D. Babcock

Wonderful Grace of Jesus
Wonderful grace of Jesus,
Greater than all my sin;
How shall my tongue describe it,
Where shall its praise begin?
Taking away my burden,
Setting my spirit free;
For the wonderful grace of Jesus reaches me.

Wonderful the matchless grace of Jesus,
Deeper than the mighty rolling sea;
Wonderful grace, all sufficient for me, for even me.
Broader than the scope of my transgressions,
Greater far than all my sin and shame,
O magnify the precious Name of Jesus.
Praise His Name!

—Haldor Lillenas

TOMBOY GRANDMAS HAVE MORE FUN

Sometimes I wonder what would have happened to me if I had been born to gender-identity-conscious parents in the twenty-first century. From as early as I can remember, I wanted to be a boy. Girl stuff was boring. Boys had more fun. I wanted to dress like a boy, wear my hair like a boy, and play boy games. My cousin Carolyn and I (who as toddlers were caught walking on the railing around my aunt and uncle's second-story balcony) gave each other boys' names; she was Charlie and I was Duane. I wasn't into anything domestic; I preferred to climb trees and jump out of them, pretending I could fly. I didn't want a frilly bed; a sleeping bag on the ground was fine with me. When all the girls in my kindergarten class were taking stupid ballet lessons, I just wanted to be outside sledding with the boys. I didn't have tea parties or play house with dolls; I pretended to ride a horse on the basement railing, and I played war with sticks for guns. My favorite sport was football, and I played tackle football with the neighborhood boys. For my ninth birthday, my Nana (proper as she was) gave me a football outfit, complete with helmet, jersey, shoulder pads, and padded pants. One year for Christmas all I wanted was boys' black buckle boots. Under the tree was a box that was a promising size and shape; I remember my annoyance when it turned out to be a dumb old piano lamp.

Did my parents wring their hands and agonize over whether to let me transition to a boy? No! They let me be me. There were sometimes arguments when Mom wanted me to wear a dress and I wanted to wear jeans, but the idea of changing gender wasn't even on the average person's radar back then. And how could I have known at age five or even fifteen—when I wanted to play on the high school football team and was thinking about becoming an astronaut—that one day I would not just play house but have a home with a husband and babies?

I am now 64 years old, have been married for 45 years, and have six children and eight grandchildren. I was not a stereotypical girl, and I'm not a stereotypical grandma. But I'm very grateful that no one ever called into question the fact that I was a girl then and I am a woman now. I still like to hike, bike, snowboard, play volleyball, and do crazy things like obstacle racing. I still get a chuckle out of the time I went snowboarding with my grandson and we were going through the terrain park, seeing how many inches of air we could get off the jumps. There I was, ready to bomb down the hill, wearing my son's borrowed goggles with holographic images of barbed wire on the lenses, and Tyler below calling, "Come on, Grandma!" Or the time I took Tyler to do F1 kart racing for his eighteenth birthday. After watching him take his turn at laps around the track, I decided that I wanted to try it myself, so I suited up and joined him for round two. We did

indeed make memories, with a broken rib—the result of crashing into the barrier—a remembrance of our experience for weeks to come. And Tyler's sister Emerson and her friend Laurille and I had a little camping adventure in the backyard that took me back to my childhood—the girls in a tent, and me between two shower curtains on the ground in the drizzle that became a downpour.

Like every single human being on the planet, I am unique, and my story is unique. I tell it not to say that others ought to be like me, but rather to give freedom to each person to be the unique and special and wonderful individual God created him or her to be.

And that dumb old piano lamp that I hoped would be boys' black buckle boots? It's still on our piano to this day—along with pictures of all our grandchildren.

FINE, HAVE IT YOUR WAY!

Two Christian leaders were engaged in a heated conflict over a decision regarding their ministry. Years earlier, one of the men had been instrumental in helping the other gain acceptance in the Christian community, and they had been ministering together in the power of the Holy Spirit for some time, but now they were unable to come to agreement. They exchanged some sharp words, and finally one man said, "*Fine*, go ahead," and the other said, "*Fine*, I will," and they parted ways.

Maybe I'm being unfair to Paul and Barnabas, but this is the way I envision their conflict over whether or not John Mark should accompany them on their second missionary journey. John Mark had been their assistant on the first journey but had left them abruptly for an undisclosed reason and gone back to Jerusalem. When it came time to go out again, Paul had no desire to take someone who had quit on them before, while Barnabas saw potential in him and wanted to give him another chance.

It does not appear that they handled it in the most godly way. There is no indication that they prayed about the situation or sought out a mediator to help them resolve it, even though they were clearly having trouble working it out themselves or even talking about it. The King James says in Acts 15:39, "the contention was so sharp between them, that they departed asunder one from the other." Another translation calls it a "sharp disagreement" that caused them to part company. The Message says that Paul "wasn't about to take along a quitter who, as soon as the going got tough, had jumped ship on them in Pamphylia. Tempers flared, and they ended up going their separate ways."

It seems that both wanted to get their own way: Barnabas insisted that they ought to take John Mark, and Paul's attitude was "It's either him or me. If you take that kid, I'm not going with you. I can't risk having someone along who needs to be babied or who might bail on us again." When they couldn't work it out, they split, and their partnership was severed.

Maybe the conversation should have gone something like this (maybe it finally did—we just don't know):

Paul: I'm afraid John Mark is not mature enough or tough enough to handle the rigors of a missionary journey.

Barnabas: But I see potential in this kid, just as I saw potential in you. Remember how I stuck up for you in Jerusalem when everybody else was afraid of you? Let's give John Mark another chance.

Paul: OK, I know that your gift is encouragement, so how about if he goes with you so you can work with him. Silas and I will go to Syria and Cilicia to minister to the Gentiles.

And they bless each other on their separate ways, trusting that God will do His work in and through each of their lives.

In any case, the bottom line is that *God was in control of the entire situation.* Though the men were both partly right and partly wrong, God absolutely knew what He was doing. Paul and Barnabas are shown as real-life, three-dimensional people; they had just helped to resolve a major controversy in the whole church earlier in Acts 15, but then they had trouble working out their own personal conflict. However, God's purposes were accomplished: The men ended up forming two teams instead of just one. Paul got the partner he needed in Silas, and their journey was an intense time of sharing the gospel with the Gentiles throughout Asia Minor and into Europe. John Mark got the mentor he needed in Barnabas, and he did indeed grow into a mature and respected believer. Perhaps his growth was even more solid under Barnabas's encouragement than it would have been under Paul's pressure. Later the men were reconciled, and Mark became Paul's "fellow worker," ministering to and with him. When Paul wrote to the Colossians, he urged them to welcome his brother Mark. In 2 Timothy, his last letter before he died, Paul said of Mark, "he is very useful to me for ministry." Paul fondly recognized Mark as being helpful not only in the ministry of the gospel, but also in ministering to Paul personally when he was in prison facing death.

Best of all, this same John Mark is the one who wrote the Gospel of Mark. God had brought him so far along that he had the wisdom and maturity to write the first record of the life of Jesus. He had studied hard and learned from Barnabas and Peter and others. Although he had been undependable and had experienced failure and rejection, he did not give up in despair, and God did not give up on him. With the help of a wise mentor, he grew into the man God intended him to be, and Christians throughout the ages have known his name and been blessed by his book.

Knowing who Mark was and who he became shows the power of God to transform. From an unstable kid he grew into a wise teacher of many. God's sovereignty in working through our sins and failures and self-centeredness is also evident. Paul and Barnabas experienced a conflict much like the ones we encounter all the time, and they muddled through it in a less-than-commendable manner. Both wanted their own way, but in the end God had His way, because He is able to use even our sins and failings to accomplish His sovereign purposes.

LET US GIVE THANKS!

Reading Ann Voskamp's book *One Thousand Gifts*, in which she describes her journey into awareness of and gratitude for God's gifts, has opened my eyes to the supreme importance of giving thanks. One reason Adam and Eve fell into sin was because they failed to be grateful for all that God had done for them and instead wanted what was not theirs to take. And what attitude in us deeply grieves God? "Although they knew God, they neither glorified him as God nor gave thanks to him, but their thinking became futile and their foolish hearts were darkened" (Rom. 1:21).

Conversely, our gratitude is like a sweet savor to God. It delights Him just as we are delighted when our children show a spirit of gratefulness. He was pleased with the thank offerings given by the Israelites from the heart. Giving thanks was one of the chief responsibilities of the Levites:

> He appointed some of the Levites to minister before the ark of the Lord, to make petition, **to give thanks**, and to praise the Lord, the God of Israel (1 Chr. 16:4).

> They were also to stand every morning **to thank and praise the Lord**. They were to do the same in the evening (1 Chr. 23:30).

The books of Chronicles speak of giving thanks more than fifteen times, six times in 1 Chronicles 16 alone. The Psalms are loaded with expressions of thanksgiving. Daniel continued to give thanks to God even when he knew it would get him thrown into the lions' den:

Now when Daniel learned that the decree had been published, he went home to his upstairs room where the windows opened toward Jerusalem. Three times a day he got down on his knees and prayed, **giving thanks to his God,** just as he had done before (Dan. 6:10).

Only one of the ten lepers who were healed came back to thank Jesus. His thanksgiving was glorifying to God, and he received the blessing of a personal commendation from Jesus.

Now one of them, when he saw that he had been healed, turned back, glorifying God with a loud voice, and he fell on his face at His feet, **giving thanks to Him**. And he was a Samaritan (Lk. 17:15-16).

Jesus gave thanks for just a few loaves and fishes, and God multiplied them abundantly:

Taking the five loaves and the two fish and looking up to heaven, **he gave thanks** and broke the loaves. Then he gave them to the disciples, and the disciples gave them to the people. They all ate and were satisfied, and the disciples picked up twelve basketfuls of broken pieces that were left over (Mt. 14:19-20).

Jesus even gave thanks as He was facing an agonizing death:

While they were eating, Jesus took bread, **gave thanks** and broke it, and gave it to his disciples, saying, "Take and eat; this is my body." Then he took the cup, **gave thanks** and offered it to them, saying, "Drink from it, all of you (Mt. 26:26-27).

And it was in the breaking of bread and giving thanks for it that the disciples recognized Him after His resurrection:

When he was at the table with them, he took bread, **gave thanks,** broke it and began to give it to them (Lk. 24:30).

Paul exhorts us over and over to give thanks, saying it is God's will for us. If you don't know what God's will in a situation is, just give thanks! You can be sure you are doing God's will when you are giving thanks. Our hearts should be filled with gratitude, as reflected by our words.

Always giving thanks to God the Father for everything, in the name of our Lord Jesus Christ (Eph. 5:20).

Do not be anxious about anything, but in everything, by prayer and petition, **with thanksgiving,** present your requests to God (Phil. 4:6).

Rooted and built up in him, strengthened in the faith as you were taught, and **overflowing with thankfulness** (Col. 2:7).

And let the peace of Christ rule in your hearts, to which indeed you were called in one body. And **be thankful.** Let the word of Christ dwell in you richly, teaching and admonishing one another in all wisdom, singing psalms and hymns and spiritual songs, **with thankfulness in your hearts to God.** And whatever you do, in word or deed, do everything in the name of the Lord Jesus, **giving thanks to God the Father** through him (Col. 3:15-17).

Devote yourselves to prayer, **being watchful and thankful** (Col. 4:2).

Give thanks in all circumstances, for this is God's will for you in Christ Jesus (1 Th. 5:18).

Ann Voskamp points out that the Greek words for *thanksgiving, grace, joy,* and *eucharist* all have the same root, *charis.* I am trying to see the connections between all those elements of the Christian life and to be more intentional about developing the habit of thanksgiving. Now that I am more alert to this theme, I'm noticing thankfulness more and more in Scripture and seeing its connection to grace and joy. And as I take the bread and cup, I find myself thanking God more and experiencing more deeply His grace and joy. I'm just beginning to scratch the surface, but I'd like to leave you with more Scriptures about this all-important theme.

Give thanks to the Lord, call on his name; make known among the nations what he has done (1 Chr. 16:8).

Give thanks to the Lord, for he is good; his love endures forever (1 Chr. 16:34).

I will praise God's name in song and **glorify him with thanksgiving** (Ps. 69:30).

But **thanks be to God!** He gives us the victory through our Lord Jesus Christ (1 Cor. 15:57).

All this is for your benefit, so that the grace that is reaching more and more people may cause **thanksgiving to overflow to the glory of God** (2 Cor. 4:15).

Thanks be to God for his indescribable gift! (2 Cor. 9:15).

Therefore, since we are receiving a kingdom that cannot be shaken, **let us be thankful,** and so worship God acceptably with reverence and awe (Heb. 12:28).

Amen! Praise and glory and wisdom and **thanks** and honor and power and strength be to our God for ever and ever. Amen! (Rev. 7:12).

Pastor Martin Rinkart wrote "Now Thank We All Our God" in the 1630s, when Germany was suffering the horrors of famine and pestilence and the Thirty Years' War. During this time, Rinkart sometimes performed as many as fifty funerals in a day. May we be able to sing these words in our own darkest hours:

Now thank we all our God with heart and hands and
    voices,
Who wondrous things has done, in whom his world
    rejoices;

Who from our mothers' arms has blessed us on our
    way
With countless gifts of love, and still is ours today.

O may this bounteous God through all our life be
    near us,
With ever joyful hearts and blessed peace to cheer us,
To keep us in his grace, and guide us when perplexed,
And free us from all ills of this world in the next.

All praise and thanks to God the Father now be given,
The Son and him who reigns with them in highest
    heaven,
The one eternal God, whom earth and heaven adore;
For thus it was, is now, and shall be evermore.

GROW IN GRACE

When I was growing up, I was not a particularly nice person. My sister Karen was the nice one—the helpful person, the Candy Striper, the kind and thoughtful one. I didn't have much patience with weak or needy people; I thought they needed to just suck it up and get a grip. When my mom would take us to visit someone at a nursing home, Karen was very sweet to the old folks, while I was thinking, "Get me outta here."

Well, God has a sense of humor. He let me become weak and needy myself. My pretense of having it all together fell apart, and I no longer tried to hide the fact that I had marriage problems and kid problems and personal problems. And gradually, over decades, God opened my eyes to the troubles of others and gave me a heart for all people. He has brought across my path many hurting people, and now, instead of thinking "Get me outta here," I can enter into their lives and offer them some of the comfort I have received from "the Father of compassion and the God of all comfort."

The first time I recall someone really opening up to me was when I greeted a young mom after church one Sunday morning. I didn't know her well, and I just said the customary "Hi, how're you doing?" She burst into tears and a whole tale tumbled out—a story of abuse by her husband and stress with her small children and struggles with money. I think the reason she felt safe with me was because it was no big secret that I had troubles of my own. I had let down my façade of pretending that I had it all together, and therefore she could be open and vulnerable with me.

Since then, there have been many more, both young and old, each with a unique life story—many filled with tragedy and hardship. I'm not any sort of therapist or counselor, just a friend. I can't fix their problems, but I can be a listener. I can't make their suffering go away, but I can serve in practical ways—whether fixing a meal, giving a ride, caring for kids, or going to court. I have little to offer in myself, but as Paul says in 2 Corinthians 1:4, God "comforts us in all our troubles, so that we can comfort those in any trouble with the comfort we ourselves receive from God." The Holy Spirit is the true Paraclete—the One who comes alongside as our helper, comforter, advocate, and guide—but each of us can serve in that role for our fellow humans.

My basic personality and identity have not changed. I'm still me. But by His grace God is little by little conforming me to the image of His Son. It's not rocket science, folks. Every human being is created by God in His image and deserves the same understanding and compassion you want for yourself. "Do to others as you would have them do to you." And remember Paul's summary of the law in Galatians 5:14: "The entire law is fulfilled in keeping this one command: 'Love your neighbor as yourself.'" Or, as an Internet meme succinctly puts it, "It's not complicated—don't be a jerk."

BITE AND DEVOUR

A seeker came to a Christian website looking for answers. His first visit turned out to be his last:

> Wow, as someone who was contemplating Christianity and directed to this website, I can say that after reading your comments to this story, I am no longer interested. So much hate for people that allegedly follow your same diety! [*sic*] No better than Sunni and Shia Muslims fighting back and forth. I thought I'd find a little more understanding and thought in the comments, but this is worse than comments on CNN or YouTube. Thank you all for being yourselves at least and showing me that Christians aren't the people in the Kirk Cameron movies.

Sadly, he was turned away from the faith not by the offense of the cross but by the ugliness he saw among professing believers.

Unfortunately this kind of interaction is not rare. On February 9, 2013, CNN published an article by John S. Dickerson entitled "My take: A word to Christians—Be nice." Dickerson was told by a well-known writer and newscaster with 1.3 million Twitter followers, some of whom claim to be "Christian," that "some of the meanest, most perverse hate-tweets he receives come from these self-proclaimed Christians."

Dickerson is *not* ashamed of the gospel, but he is embarrassed to be associated with some of those who represent Christ:

These are the moments when it's embarrassing to be a Christian. I'm not embarrassed to believe the extravagant claims of Christianity: that Christ was born to a virgin, died for our sins, physically rose from the grave and is returning to rule the world. But I am embarrassed to be associated with some of the people who claim his name.

Dickerson acknowledges that the bad reputation of American evangelical Christians is due in part to persecution for preaching the gospel, but he is concerned about the disrepute that we bring upon ourselves. He quotes 1 Peter 4:

> If you are insulted for the name of Christ, you are blessed, because the Spirit of glory and of God rests upon you. But let none of you suffer as a murderer or a thief or an evildoer or as a meddler (14-15).

In other words, if you are treated with contempt because you proclaim the name of Christ, you are blessed. But if you suffer "persecution" just for being a jerk, don't blame it on the gospel. Dickerson notes that "the word 'meddler' means busybody: someone who inserts himself into matters that are not his own. Might this include some people involved in the Twitter, Facebook and 'comments' showdowns of our day?"

It can be painful to be the brunt of attacks against one's character, and it can be costly in one's personal life. But the greater concern is for the name of Christ and the well-being of His Body and the proclamation of the gospel. Paul warns in Galatians 5:15 not to "bite and devour one another." Biting and devouring is the work of the enemy, who seeks to divide and destroy us:

> Your adversary, the devil, prowls around like a roaring lion, seeking someone to devour (1 Pet. 5:8).

John has stern words for those who verbally bite and devour their brothers and sisters, which is tantamount to hating them:

Whoever says he is in the light and hates his brother is still in darkness…. Whoever hates his brother is in the darkness and walks in the darkness, and does not know where he is going, because the darkness has blinded his eyes…. If anyone says, "I love God," yet hates his brother, he is a liar. For anyone who does not love his brother, whom he has seen, cannot love God, whom he has not seen (1 Jn. 2:9, 11; 4:20).

Dickerson quotes James 3 and Matthew 12 to urge Christians not to bite and devour one another and to remind them that they will have to give account for their words:

With the tongue we praise our Lord and father, and with it we curse men, who have been made in God's likeness. Out of the same mouth come praise and cursing. My brothers, *this should not be* (Js. 3:9, 10).

For out of the overflow of the heart the mouth speaks. The good man brings good things out of the good stored up in him, and the evil man brings evil things out of the evil stored up in him. But I tell you that men will have to give account on the day of judgment for every careless word they have spoken (Mt. 12:34-36).

Then Dickerson asks,

If we will give account for every careless word spoken, might we also give account for every careless comment typed or tweeted?

Good question.

FRUITFUL WORDS

The essay "Bite and Devour" (page 34) urges Christians *not* to do what Paul warned against in Galatians 5:15. Here are some of Paul's positive admonitions in Galatians and other epistles about what we *ought* to do and be.

In Galatians 5 Paul goes on to name the works of the flesh and the fruit of the Spirit. Among the works of the flesh are "rivalries, dissensions, and divisions." The fruit of the Spirit stands in stark contrast:

> But the fruit of the Spirit is love, joy, peace, patience, kindness, goodness, faithfulness, gentleness, and self-control (22-23).

These are the qualities that should characterize not only our speech, but all of our actions. Those who belong to Jesus put to death the works of the flesh and live by the Spirit. If someone does need to be corrected, it should be done "in a spirit of gentleness" with the goal of restoring the person.

A friend shared this acronym that her mom taught her. It reminds us to "think" about our words *before* we speak or write them:

T—Is it **true?**
H—Is it **helpful?**
I—Is it **impartial?**
N—Is it **necessary?**
K—Is it **kind?**

If we were to ask ourselves these questions before letting our words fly, we would do less damage and bring more healing.

Paul's other epistles give further advice about the use of the tongue:

Speak the truth in love (Eph. 4:15).

Speak only what is good for building up, as fits the occasion, that it may give grace to those who hear (Eph. 4:30).

Do all things without grumbling or disputing, that you may be blameless and innocent, children of God without blemish in the midst of a crooked and twisted generation, among whom you shine as lights in the world (Phil. 2:14-15).

Let your reasonableness be known to everyone (Phil. 4:5).

Put on then, as God's chosen ones, holy and beloved, compassionate hearts, kindness, humility, meekness, and patience, bearing with one another and, if one has a complaint against another, forgiving each other; as the Lord has forgiven you, so you also must forgive. And above all these put on love, which binds every-thing together in perfect harmony (Col. 3:12-14).

As James says, none of us can completely control our words:

For we all stumble in many ways. And if anyone does not stumble in what he says, he is a perfect man, able also to bridle his whole body (Js. 3:2).

But our goal should be to make all our words gracious and pleasing to God:

Let your speech always be gracious, seasoned with salt, so that you may know how you ought to answer each person (Col. 4:6).

THE ADVIL SEASON

One year when my son Daniel was little, his class made a Christmas craft—little jars with one M&M® for each day of Advent. Dan showed me his jar and explained, "You get to eat one M&M each day of Advil."

Does the time of preparation for Christmas ever feel more like the Advil season than the Advent season? Do you ever get that frazzled feeling thinking of all the things you have to do? Do you find yourself getting scattered in so many directions that you don't accomplish much of anything? Or, on the other hand, do you get so task-oriented that you become inflexible and fail to meet unanticipated needs that arise?

When you read the Gospels, you never get the sense that Jesus was frazzled or scattered or inflexible. He was incredibly focused, yet fully flexible. He had a clear sense of purpose for His whole life, and for each day. Yet He never made the mistake that we often do of getting so stuck on our own agenda that we become blind to what is really important.

When Jesus purposed to go to the home of Jairus, it was urgent because Jairus's daughter was dying. Yet when an anonymous woman in the crowd touched His coat, Jesus stopped to minister to her, never losing sight of Jairus's need. Another time He invited the disciples to come away with Him to get some rest, but His compassion for the multitude caused Him to change His plans. As the Father led, Jesus met the needs of the people who crossed His path—a dying girl, a bleeding woman, a demon-possessed child, a man with a withered hand, a grieving mother, a blind man, a deaf man, a dead man, a leper, a paralytic, an adulteress, the hungry and hurting multitudes.

Yet for all His flexibility, *nothing* could deter the Savior from the supremely important task for which the Father sent Him. Everything He did was leading ultimately to the cross, and when the time was right, He resolutely went to Jerusalem to fulfill that purpose.

All through His ministry, Jesus knew just what to do each day, each moment. How did He do it? Just because Jesus was God didn't mean that He could simply coast along on His deity. In His humanity He had to maintain His relationship with the Father just like we do, and we have the record of His life so we can learn how He did it.

Jesus perfectly practiced something that we can do too: He knew how to walk in the Spirit. From His times alone with the Father, Jesus knew how to hear His voice and understand His will. He was aware of what God wanted Him to do each moment, and He always did it. He never gave in to external pressures and demands—and there were many on Him—but He always flowed with the inner leading of the Holy Spirit.

To follow in the footsteps of Jesus may seem like an impossible goal. But it is God's desire for us, and He has given us the Holy Spirit to enable us. In Romans 8 Paul talks about life through the Spirit. He urges us to be set free by the Spirit of life, to walk according to the Spirit, to live according to the Spirit, to set our minds on the Spirit, to let the Spirit of God dwell in us, to receive life in our mortal bodies through His Spirit, to put to death the deeds of the body by the Spirit, to be led by the Spirit of God, to listen to the Spirit bearing witness that we are children of God and heirs with Christ, and to allow the Spirit to help us in our weakness and intercede for us.

I can't tell you exactly how to walk in the Spirit, because I'm still learning myself. But I can invite you to keep on searching the Scriptures, getting to know Jesus who is our model for living, and learning how to listen, as He did, to the Father's voice. We can purpose in our hearts to be controlled not by external pressures or guilt or other people's demands or our own compulsions or society's expectations or anything else except the Spirit of God. Then we too can experience the beautiful balance that Jesus had.

The Christmas season may be the most challenging time of the year for many of us to achieve that balance. The beginning of Advent is a good time to purpose to resist the pressures of the world and to walk in the Spirit. At the end of His life Jesus could say in John 17:4, "I have brought you glory on earth by completing the work you gave me to do." If we make it our goal each day to complete the work God gives us—and only what He gives us—then we will have time and energy to do what needs to be done, and at the end of our lives we will be able to say when we stand before God that we brought Him glory on earth by completing the work He gave us to do.

BANKRUPTCY OR PROSPERITY?
LESSONS FROM A CORPORATE COLLAPSE

The company I used to work for filed for Chapter 11 bankruptcy because of a slight budget problem: *three billion dollars* of debt. Founded nearly two centuries ago, the company was once prestigious and well-respected, but no longer. The news hit home to me because of the personal connection, and it made me think about how to avoid on a personal level what happened to this company on a massive scale.

There are multiple causes for this epic downfall, but the company spokesman's reasons are code for "it's somebody else's fault":

"recession-driven increases"—
"It's the economy's fault."

"purchase deferrals" by the states—
"It's the states' fault."

"lack of anticipated federal stimulus support"—
"It's the federal government's fault."

"the global financial crisis"—
"It's the whole world's fault."

The book of James has a lot to say about how to avoid such a catastrophe, starting with being honest about our own sins and taking **personal responsibility** for our actions. He says in 5:16, "Confess your sins to each other"—to acknowledge that we have done wrong. We are not to put the blame on others but rather take a hard look at ourselves and recognize our own shortcomings.

42

It takes **sincere humility** to admit personal failure. James warns against pride and calls his readers to humble themselves:

God opposes the proud but gives grace to the humble (4:6).

Humble yourselves before the Lord, and he will lift you up (4:10).

Humility comes from **godly wisdom**. James exhorts us not to trust human wisdom but rather to acquire the wisdom that comes from above:

If any of you lacks wisdom, he should ask God, who gives generously to all without finding fault, and it will be given to him (1:5).

Who is wise and understanding among you? Let him show it by his good life, by deeds done in the humility that comes from wisdom (3:13).

The wisdom that comes from heaven is first of all pure; then peace-loving, considerate, submissive, full of mercy and good fruit, impartial and sincere (3:17).

Those of us in the trenches of the company—the peons with no voice—could see the foolishness of many of the decisions made by management, like acquiring other companies right and left and trying to grow too fast. James warns against such greed and ambition and urges instead that we practice **faithful perseverance** in doing what is right:

If you harbor bitter envy and selfish ambition in your hearts, do not boast about it or deny the truth (3:14).

For where you have envy and selfish ambition, there you find disorder and every evil practice (3:16).

Blessed is the one who perseveres under trial because, having stood the test, that person will receive the crown of life that the Lord has promised to those who love him (1:12).

Selfish ambition can also lead to exploiting people, another evil that James decries. He forcefully denounces the rich who abuse the poor, in particular, employers who fail to **treat workers fairly**:

> Now listen, you rich people, weep and wail because of the misery that is coming upon you (5:1).

> Look! The wages you failed to pay the workmen who mowed your fields are crying out against you. The cries of the harvesters have reached the ears of the Lord Almighty (5:4).

Finally, James cautions against making grandiose plans with no thought for God. Rather, we should **submit our plans and our future to God's will**:

> Now listen, you who say, "Today or tomorrow we will go to this or that city, spend a year there, carry on business and make money." Why, you do not even know what will happen tomorrow (4:13-14).

> Instead, you ought to say, "If it is the Lord's will, we will live and do this or that" (4:15).

These are just a few of the principles packed into the book of James. They hold true on a corporate as well as a personal level. Violating these principles can lead to financial bankruptcy—as in the case of my former employer—and even worse, to moral and spiritual bankruptcy. Heed James's words to avoid such a disaster!

UNITED WE STAND

In the wake of the 2013 Marathon bombing, the city of Boston pulled together in a remarkable way. The moment the first bomb went off, courageous people rushed in to help the wounded. Exhausted runners summoned up more strength to run to hospitals to donate blood. Law enforcement officers risked their lives to capture the suspects. Money poured in to assist the victims in their recovery.

In fact, there was a worldwide outpouring of support for Boston. Sports rivalries, personal animosity, and even national hostilities were set aside, at least temporarily, to show solidarity with a grieving city. The spirit of the Marathon itself—the spirit of camaraderie and unity—carried over into the days following the tragedy.

Photo by Beth Murphy

For a time, the city became the kind of community we all want to be part of. Unfortunately, some look for acceptance and bonding in the wrong places—in a gang or a group of drug buddies or a terrorist cell. But there are many legitimate ways to find community and fellowship—a family, a sports team, a workplace, a knitting circle, a professional society, a fraternity or sorority, a charitable organization, a cultural community, a book club, a bowling league. And God has given us the Body of Christ to satisfy the longing for fellowship that He has planted in us and also to be a lighthouse pointing the way to the Kingdom of love and fellowship that He is establishing.

Philippians 2 describes the kind of community that God invites us to be part of. The first part of the passage talks about the qualities we should be developing as we live with one another:

> So if there is any encouragement in Christ, any comfort from love, any participation in the Spirit, any affection and sympathy, complete my joy by being of the same mind, having the same love, being in full accord and of one mind. Do nothing from selfish ambition or conceit, but in humility count others more significant than yourselves. Let each of you look not only to his own interests, but also to the interests of others (vv. 1-4).

Can you imagine if we fully put into practice the qualities and actions described here: encouragement, comfort, love, affection, sympathy, joy, unity, love, humility (no selfish ambition or conceit), looking out for others? Our model is Jesus Himself:

> Have this mind among yourselves, which is yours in Christ Jesus, who, though he was in the form of God, did not count equality with God a thing to be grasped, but emptied himself, by taking the form of a servant, being born in the likeness of men. And being found in human form, he humbled himself by becoming obedient to the point of death, even death on a cross (vv. 5-8).

He is the embodiment of humility and sacrifice. He is equal with God the Father, but He gave up everything to come to earth as a servant and even to die for us. And the final result will be that He is exalted above all and will draw us into full communion with Him:

Therefore God has highly exalted him and bestowed on him the name that is above every name, so that at the name of Jesus every knee should bow, in heaven and on earth and under the earth, and every tongue confess that Jesus Christ is Lord, to the glory of God the Father (vv. 9-11).

As Paul says in Ephesians 1, God's purpose for the fullness of time is to unite all things in Christ (vv. 9-10). Philippians 2 tells us how to live in the meantime—how to live out our faith and live into the unity that will one day be a complete reality.

In time, life in Boston went back to what is more normal: ordinary violence kept happening, neighbors fought with each other again, and the Yankees went back to hating the Red Sox. But we have the promise that God will one day fully bring in His Kingdom of love, justice, unity, and peace. If you know Jesus Christ, you have this hope in you, and you want to live it out in your daily life, with Jesus as your model. As John says,

Martin Richard, the youngest Marathon bombing victim. "No more hurting people. Peace."

See what kind of love the Father has given to us, that we should be called children of God; and so we are. The reason why the world does not know us is that it did not know him. Beloved, we are God's children now, and what we will be has not yet appeared; but we know that when he appears we shall be like him, because we shall see him as he is. And everyone who thus hopes in him purifies himself as he is pure (1 Jn. 3:1-3).

If you don't know Him but you feel a stirring in your heart to want to be part of this kind of community, come to Him. Please forgive us Christians for failing so often to practice the kind of love and humility we are called to as followers of Christ—as John says, we are not yet what we should be! But one day God's Kingdom of peace will be a full reality, and in the meantime we can get a foretaste of it by living out our calling as children of God and lights in the world (Phil. 2:15).

ELISABETH ELLIOT JOINS
THE GREAT CLOUD OF WITNESSES

On June 23, 2015, legendary missionary Elisabeth Elliot Gren was laid to rest. As a shy and humble person, she would probably resist the term "legendary" to describe herself, but she was a true pioneer in bringing the gospel to the unreached peoples of Ecuador.

Her initial work as a missionary may have been regarded by some as a failure. In 1956, her husband, Jim Elliot, and four other men were murdered by members of the fierce and violent Waorani tribe they were trying to reach with the gospel, leaving five grieving widows and nine fatherless children. It seemed that the effort was doomed, but God had plans to use the martyrs' deaths in ways that no one could have imagined at the time.

By faith Elisabeth stayed in Ecuador with her little daughter, Valerie. Instead of seeking revenge, as the Waorani would have done, she still longed to bring the love of God to them. She developed a friendship with two Waorani women and learned the language from them. Just two years after the tragedy, Elisabeth and three-year-old Valerie went to live among the very people who had killed their husband and father. As she communicated the gospel of Jesus Christ to them in words and in sacrificial love, the hoped-for day did come when they joined her in praise to the Savior.

Returning to the States after her time in Ecuador, Elisabeth shared her wisdom and experience through writing and speaking. She was well acquainted with grief, as she walked through the valley again when she lost her second husband,

Addison Leitch. In addition to suffering, her themes included trusting God and building strong Christian families. And photographer Cornell Capa, who chronicled the massacre in Ecuador and its aftermath for *Life* magazine, discovered another key theme that undergirded her life. He asked the young widows why their husbands went into that hostile territory in the first place. The one-word answer was "obedience." They were all committed to following God no matter what the cost.

By faith Elisabeth handled the dementia that struck her in her later years just as she faced the other losses in her life: with surrender and trust. She knew that fiery trials are to be expected in the Christian life and that they are opportunities to partake in Christ's sufferings:

> Beloved, think it not strange concerning the fiery trial which is to try you, as though some strange thing happened unto you: But rejoice, inasmuch as ye are partakers of Christ's sufferings; that, when his glory shall be revealed, ye may be glad also with exceeding joy (1 Pet. 4:12-13 KJV).

As her son-in-law explained at her funeral, she believed that, when put on a scale, "our troubles become like feathers" in comparison to the weight of glory to come:

> For our light affliction, which is but for a moment, worketh for us a far more exceeding and eternal weight of glory; While we look not at the things which are seen, but at the things which are not seen: for the things which are seen are temporal; but the things which are not seen are eternal (2 Cor. 4:17-18 KJV).

She called to mind the promise of Isaiah 43:2 and the words of "How Firm a Foundation":

> When thou passest through the waters, I will be with thee; and through the rivers, they shall not overflow thee: when thou walkest through the fire, thou shalt not be burned; neither shall the flame kindle upon thee.

When through fiery trials thy pathways shall lie,
My grace, all sufficient, shall be thy supply;
The flame shall not hurt thee; I only design
Thy dross to consume, and thy gold to refine.

Another favorite song was "He Giveth More Grace," by Annie J. Flint:

He giveth more grace as our burdens grow greater,
He sendeth more strength as our labors increase;
To added afflictions He addeth His mercy,
To multiplied trials He multiplies peace.

His love has no limits, His grace has no measure,
His power no boundary known unto men;
For out of His infinite riches in Jesus
He giveth, and giveth, and giveth again.

By faith Elisabeth walked with God throughout her life and was received into that great cloud of witnesses. Her brother Dr. David Howard read Revelation 14:13:

Blessed are the dead which die in the Lord from henceforth: Yea, saith the Spirit, that they may rest from their labours; and their works do follow them.

Elisabeth is now resting from all her labors, but her words and works will continue to testify of her Savior.

Nearly a year after Elisabeth's death I saw her husband, Lars. I commented about how difficult the last year without her must have been, and he said, "What has helped in this past year is the gift of the last morning which the two caregivers and I had with her as she crossed into life evermore." God is faithful in sorrow, and He will be faithful to reunite them again.

CLASS REUNION COMING UP?
JUST DO IT

Maybe you would just as soon forget high school, or maybe you put it behind you long ago, or maybe you walked through it in a drug-induced haze and never remembered much of it in the first place. But whatever your experience, those were formative years in your life, and the people around you at that time were instrumental in shaping you into the person you are today.

If you have the opportunity to reconnect with some of those people at a class reunion, I recommend that you go for it. If your instinctive reaction is to say no, I'm sure you can think of many reasons why not to do it. But give yourself a chance to consider it. If any of the following objections spring to mind, give some thought to how you can overcome them:

- "I don't remember anybody, and nobody will remember me."

Plan to introduce yourself. Get reacquainted. Or talk with someone you never knew. Take the initiative; it may be easier to connect than you expect it to be.

- "I was never in the popular crowd."

There may still be traces of the high school cliques, but you may be surprised at how divisions have dissolved and different groups blend. Reach out to someone who was in another crowd.

- "I've gained too much weight."

Guaranteed there will be others who feel the same. Make it a goal to put them at ease.

- "I have aged more than everybody else."

Life has happened to you. You have matured, and you have wisdom to share. Your gray hair and wrinkles are nothing to be ashamed of.

- "I haven't been successful in my career."

There will always be some who are still playing the game of comparing and disparaging, but many have moved beyond it. Be honest. People will appreciate your authenticity and will be more likely to be vulnerable themselves.

- "I'm embarrassed about my family situation."

You may be divorced, have a prodigal child, have lost a child to suicide, or have experienced countless other types of sorrow in your family. As with their careers, some people would like you to think that their families are perfect. Don't believe it.

- "I'm at a different place religiously and politically."

Listen respectfully as others tell their views; they may be more willing to listen as you tell what you are passionate about.

- "It's too far away/too expensive/too complicated logistically."

You may not be able to make it this time, but you know when it will happen again. Plan ahead!

- "Our class doesn't do reunions."

Plan one yourself! Find a friend, brainstorm together, choose a date, and spread the word. With social media it's easier than ever to find lost classmates. The organizers of our reunion had a very successful plan for the weekend: An informal get-together with drinks and snacks at a bar Friday night was a good ice-breaker. One of our favorite teachers gave us a tour of the school on Saturday morning. Saturday evening we had dinner at a nice restaurant. A bring-your-own-lunch family picnic on Sunday is a fun, low-budget way to wrap up the weekend.

So take a deep breath, swallow your pride, strip away the pretenses, spend some time with the people you grew up with, and grow with them again.

WHO AM I AND WHO WILL I BE?

My son Alex, who is a doctor, gave me the book *The Man Who Mistook His Wife for a Hat,* by British neurologist Oliver Sacks.[1] Dr. Sacks tells the stories of people with strange neurological disorders that alter their mind, body, perception, and personality. One man lost all memory of events past the end of World War II and for the next few decades imagined that he was still a young seaman. "The Disembodied Lady" lost her sense of the relative positions of her own body parts and had to use her eyes and concentrate intensely to "find" and move her limbs. The man in the title was an accomplished musician who was robbed of the ability to recognize faces:

> Not only did Dr. P. increasingly fail to see faces, but he saw faces when there were no faces to see: genially, Magoo-like, when in the street he might pat the heads of water hydrants and parking meters, taking these to be the heads of children.

Dr. Sacks tells these stories with great respect for the personhood of each individual. In the words of the book cover, "If inconceivably strange, in Dr. Sacks's splendid and sympathetic telling these people remain deeply human." Another doctor, neurosurgeon Paul Kalanithi,[2] expressed this same respect for his patients' personhood in his book *When Breath Becomes Air:* "The call to protect life—and not merely life but another's identity, it is perhaps not too much to say another's soul—was obvious in its sacredness. Before operating on a patient's brain, I realized, I must first understand his mind: his identity, his values, what makes his life worth living."

The stories in Dr. Sacks's book echoed a theme that has become key in my life: that every human being is created in the image of God and has immeasurable value in His eyes, no matter how much that image is distorted by sin, disease, or impairment. Reading the book and thinking what it would be like to face severe neurological deficits made me reflect on the question of identity and what it means to be human. What makes us who we are? Where do we get our personhood?

I thought about the question "Who am I?" I am a daughter. (I have been since the moment I was conceived!) I am a granddaughter. I am a sister. I am a niece. I am an aunt. I am a wife. I am a mother. I am a grandmother. I am a neighbor. I am a friend. I am a classmate. I am a writer. I am a colleague. I am a teammate. I am a child of God. I am a member of the Body of Christ.

As I thought about who I am, I realized how much of my identity is derived from my *relationships*. I have been shaped by all my interactions with other people—from the family I know most intimately to the colleagues I know only through email and the people I cross paths with and never even know their names. Our identity is inextricably linked to all the people who have influenced our lives in ways great and small.

I have also been thinking about the question "Who will I be?" Not just over the next few years or until the end of my life, but beyond the end of my earthly life, when mortality is "swallowed up by life." I know we will get new bodies and be transformed into the image of Christ. I believe our core identity will still exist in a recognizable form. And the relationships that have helped create my identity will still exist too.

Each person in our lives is special to us and to God. A book I read to my little granddaughter captures the uniqueness and value of every human life, as every new parent looking into his or her baby's eyes knows:

On the night you were born,
the moon smiled with such wonder
that the stars peeked in to see you
and the night wind whispered,
"Life will never be the same."
Because there had never been anyone like you—
ever in the world.[3]

And a poem by Henry Scott Holland (1847–1918), Regius Professor of Divinity at the University of Oxford, expresses the Christian's hope that after death we will still be who we are—people of great value to one another and to God:

Death Is Nothing At All
Death is nothing at all.
I have only slipped away to the next room.
I am I and you are you.
Whatever we were to each other,
That, we still are.

Call me by my old familiar name.
Speak to me in the easy way
which you always used.
Put no difference into your tone.
Wear no forced air of solemnity or sorrow.

Laugh as we always laughed
at the little jokes we enjoyed together.
Play, smile, think of me. Pray for me.
Let my name be ever the household word that it
    always was.
Let it be spoken without effect.
Without the trace of a shadow on it.

Life means all that it ever meant.
It is the same that it ever was.
There is absolute unbroken continuity.
Why should I be out of mind
because I am out of sight?

I am but waiting for you.
For an interval.
Somewhere. Very near.
Just around the corner.

All is well.

---

[1] Sacks's book *Awakenings* was the basis for the 1990 movie of the same name starring Robin Williams and Robert DeNiro. It is the account of survivors of the 1920s encephalitic lethargica ("sleepy sickness") epidemic. The disease attacked their brain and left them unable to speak or move, but in the late 1960s Dr. Sacks discovered that the drug L-DOPA could "awaken" them from their statue-like condition, with dramatic effects. His treatment of them is characterized by sensitivity to the personhood and feelings of each victim. Dr. Sacks passed away in August 2015, at age 82.

[2] Kalanithi, Paul. *When Breath Becomes Air*, 2016. Dr. Kalanithi's book is a moving memoir of his life and his battle against lung cancer. He passed away in March 2015, before his thirty-eighth birthday.

[3] Tillman, Nancy. *On the Night You Were Born*

JOY IS A CHOICE, PART 1

In the summer of 1989 I had the opportunity to go on a wilderness trip with La Vida, a Christian Outward-Bound-style program. We spent eight days camping, hiking, and canoeing in the Adirondack Mountains of New York. One of the themes of our time was "Choose Joy"—the idea that joy is not something that happens to us when all the circumstances are right, but rather a choice that we can make at any time. We don't have to be lying on the beach in the warm sun with a good book; we can be lying on the ground in a soggy sleeping bag in the pouring rain.

Toward the end of our trip we each went on a solo, a 36-hour period of being alone in the woods with no food, no flashlight, no fire—just the clothes on our backs, a jug of water, a sleeping bag, and a Bible, notebook, and pen. During that time I decided to explore the theme of joy in the book of Philippians. Paul knew about finding joy in difficult situations; he understood that real joy is not dependent on circumstances or emotions; it is a choice. His letter is full of references to joy despite the fact that he was suffering in prison.

Here are some of the practical choices we can make to free ourselves from hindrances to joy:

1. **Rather than complain about my circumstances, be content in my circumstances and thank God that He is working in my life.**

   He who began a good work in you will carry it on to completion (1:6).

   Do everything without complaining or arguing (2:14).

59

I have learned to be content whatever the circumstances.... I have learned the secret of being content
in any and every situation (4:11-12).

Paul says to "do everything without complaining or
arguing so that you may become blameless and pure, children
of God...[who] shine like stars in the universe" (2:14-15).
Complaining is a very natural human reaction; not complaining really sets apart the children of God and makes for
inward and outward peace.

Paul had learned to rise above his circumstances instead
of letting them rule him. He said, "I have learned to be content whatever the circumstances.... I have learned the secret
of being content in any and every situation" (4:11-12). He was
not held captive by the whims of circumstances but was able
to remain steady through ups and downs. I can also *learn*
(through a process, not an overnight transformation) to be
content with the way God has made me, where He has put
me, and what He has given to me.

It is also reassuring that God is working in my life
through all my circumstances. "Being confident of this, that
He who began a good work in you will carry it on to completion until the day of Christ Jesus" (1:6). In everything that
happens God is at work to mold me into the image of His
Son. Sometimes it's like labor in childbirth—the more it
hurts, the more is happening inside. Maybe the results aren't
immediately visible, but the work is progressing toward
completion nevertheless.

2. Rather than envy others or compete with them, be united with them, love them, esteem them, help them.

Make my joy complete by being like-minded, having
the same love, being one in spirit and purpose. Do
nothing out of selfish ambition or vain conceit, but in
humility consider others better than yourselves. Each
of you should look not only to your own interests but
also to the interests of others (2:2-4).

Sometimes I find myself looking at my friends and feeling very inadequate; they seem to be so much more successful/ spiritual/satisfied, etc. Then I realize that I'm not _____ or _____ (fill in the blanks with the names of super-together people); I'm *me*. God doesn't want me comparing myself with my friends; I should have the true humility that allows me to see myself accurately, to think of myself with sober judgment, as Paul says in Romans 12:3, and not be intimidated by others. We're all on the same team and I should rejoice in others' strengths and help them in their weaknesses.

The flip side of comparing and feeling inferior is comparing and feeling superior ("vain conceit"), which is equally destructive. As Paul instructed in Romans 12:3, "do not think of yourself more highly than you ought." I picture Euodia and Syntyche, who are addressed in Philippians 4, as strong-minded and opinionated women who loved the Lord but thought their own ideas about how the church should operate were the only way to go. Paul urged them to come together in unity to work cooperatively rather than competitively for the well-being of the whole body.

God longs for us to have "encouragement from being united with Christ," "comfort from his love," "fellowship with the Spirit," "tenderness and compassion" (2:1). Paul says that the path to complete joy is being "like-minded, having the same love, being one in spirit and purpose" (2:2) and looking to the interests of others (2:4). We should be looking for ways to build others up, not wasting energy trying to keep up with them or prove ourselves better.

3. **Rather than boast about what I have achieved or hang onto what I have attained, consider it all loss compared to knowing Christ.**

But whatever was to my profit I now consider loss for the sake of Christ. What is more, I consider every-thing a loss compared to the surpassing greatness of knowing Christ Jesus my Lord, for whose sake I have lost all things (3:7-8).

Paul had plenty to brag about—pedigree, titles, honors, achievements—but he counts it all of no value. He could have had worldly wealth and success, but he considers all of it "rubbish." His goal is to be found in Christ, "not having a righteousness of my own…, but that which is through faith in Christ" (3:9). His overarching purpose is "to know Christ and the power of his resurrection and the fellowship of sharing in his sufferings, becoming like him in his death, and so, somehow, to attain to the resurrection from the dead" (3:10-11).

I shouldn't be puffed up about what I do or proud of what I have; God is the one who enables, and it is for His glory, not mine. As Paul prayed, we should be "filled with the fruit of righteousness that comes through Jesus Christ—to the glory and praise of God" (1:11). I will find more joy just knowing Christ, seeking God's glory rather than my own.

4. **Rather than being consumed with guilt about what I have or haven't done, receive God's forgiveness and get on with my life.**

    Forgetting what is behind and straining toward what is ahead, I press on toward the goal to win the prize for which God has called me heavenward in Christ Jesus (3:13-14).

    I could spend the rest of my life wallowing in guilt over what I've done or failed to do, but it would be a waste. Jesus died to free us from bondage to sin and guilt.

    Paul had done some pretty rotten things in his life, and he could have held onto the guilt and been paralyzed into inaction. But he learned to forget what is behind and press on toward the goal of pleasing God and doing His will. Being released from the guilt of our past by God's forgiveness allows us to experience His joy now and to get on with the work to which He has called us.

5. **Rather than dwell on what I am suffering, see how God can use it to further the gospel, and be thankful that I can share suffering with Christ.**

Now I want you to know, brothers, that what has happened to me has really served to advance the gospel.... Because of my chains, most of the brothers in the Lord have been encouraged to speak the word of God more courageously and fearlessly (1:12, 14).

The important thing is that in every way,... Christ is preached. And because of this I rejoice. Yes, and I will continue to rejoice (1:18).

It has been granted to you on behalf of Christ...to suffer for him (1:29).

Paul had lost his freedom and was living under miserable conditions in prison, but what was important to him was that more people were learning about Jesus. Many realized that he was in chains because of his faith (1:13), and they were drawn to the gospel. His courage in the face of suffering also emboldened other believers to preach the word more courageously (1:14). And as long as Jesus' name was being lifted up, Paul was full of joy (1:18).

It is a privilege to be able to suffer with and for Christ (1:29). As we identify with Him in suffering, we are drawn closer to Him and we have the joy of knowing that our witness is bringing honor to Him. And Paul says that it is through sharing in His suffering and death that we will also share in the resurrection from the dead (3:10-11). What greater joy than knowing we will be raised from the dead to share His life forever!

See Part 2 (page 64) for more principles for joy.

JOY IS A CHOICE, PART 2

One of the hallmarks of the Christian is joy. Part 1 (page 59) presented five choices that we can make in order to experience the joy of the Lord. Here are five more principles from the book of Philippians.

6. **Rather than getting frustrated or angry with others, take the opportunity to intercede for them.**

I thank my God every time I remember you. In all my prayers for all of you, I always pray with joy (1:3-4).

And this is my prayer: that your love may abound more and more in knowledge and depth of insight, so that you may be able to discern what is best and may be pure and blameless until the day of Christ, filled with the fruit of righteousness that comes through Jesus Christ—to the glory and praise of God (1:9-11).

Many of us have a tendency to hang onto anger, to nurse it and to justify ourselves in holding something against someone else. It may feel good momentarily, but anger can be a destructive emotion, eating us up without solving anything. We would be more joyful if we could learn to take our feeling of irritation toward another as a cue to pray for that person. Praying for others can soften your heart toward them and help you to see them through God's eyes.

Paul must have faced many frustrations in dealing with all kinds of sinful, broken people. Some Christians were even trying to hurt him deliberately; he said that such people "preach Christ out of selfish ambition, not sincerely, supposing that they can stir up trouble for me while I am in chains" (1:17). But he did not harbor bitterness against them, and he even found joy in the fact that Christ was being preached (1:18). He obeyed the words of Jesus to "pray for those who mistreat you" (Lk. 6:28). Most of his epistles begin with prayer for the spiritual growth of the people, and it gave him great joy to know that God was answering those prayers.

7. **Rather than being a workaholic or a control freak or just doing nothing, do what I can and trust God to do the rest.**

Therefore, my dear friends, as you have always obeyed,... continue to work out your salvation with fear and trembling. For it is God who works in you to will and to act according to his good purpose (2:12-13).

I can do everything through him who gives me strength (4:13).

It can be very tricky to keep in balance what I should do and what I should wait on God to do. Sometimes I expect God to do what I ought to do, and sometimes I try to plow through in my own strength without recognizing my dependence on Him. Paul tells us to "work out" our salvation as God works in us. We don't have to work *for* our salvation—it is a gift given freely by God's grace—but we do have to work it out. We have a day-to-day responsibility to act in ways that will promote our sanctification, yet at the same time, God is the one who is working in us. He gives the ability and even the willingness, though we have to open ourselves up to be able and willing.

As we faced the portages on our canoe trip, sometimes I felt as if I couldn't do it (or didn't want to). It seemed like it would be nice to plop down at the beginning and pray, "Lord, levitate me and my stuff to the other side." But God doesn't do for us the things He has given us the ability to do ourselves. Maybe I didn't have the strength to do it all, but I *could* pick up my pack and put one foot in front of the other, and in the process I found strength to take more steps. Maybe I couldn't carry a canoe all the way, but I could do it part way, then rest, and then carry it some more.

Similarly, in life's everyday challenges, we have to use the ability God has given us and trust Him for what is beyond us. If I'm looking for a job I can't expect God to write my resume and make the contacts, but I *can* expect Him to guide me along the way and weave together the right set of circumstances. And in the process of doing what I *can* do, God gives the ability to do what I thought I couldn't do. Working out my salvation means I work in His strength, not my own, and I let God be in control rather than trying to manipulate circumstances myself. It gives a sense of peace and joy to know that I have done my best and left the rest to Him.

8. **Rather than waste energy worrying, bring everything to the Lord with prayer and thanksgiving.**

> Do not be anxious about anything, but in everything, by prayer and petition, with thanksgiving, present your requests to God. And the peace of God, which transcends all understanding, will guard your hearts and your minds in Christ Jesus (4:6-7).

Fear and worry can immobilize a person and strip him or her of joy. There is plenty to worry about in this world, but God doesn't want us to drain ourselves worrying, but rather to trust Him and to be intentionally thankful. We are commanded not to be anxious about *anything.* But what do we do with the feelings of worry and anxiety that inevitably assault us when trials come?

Prayer is the most productive outlet for fear and worry, and the promised result is a profound peace: "The peace of God, which transcends all understanding, will guard your hearts and your minds in Christ Jesus." Knowing that I have brought my cares to the Lord, that He has heard me and is in control, enables me to rest in Him with the tranquility of a sleeping child.

9. **Rather than thinking about the negative, discipline my mind to dwell on the positive.**

Finally, brothers, whatever is true, whatever is noble, whatever is right, whatever is pure, whatever is lovely, whatever is admirable—if anything is excellent or praiseworthy—think about such things (4:8).

What I allow my mind to dwell on will be very influential in my whole outlook. As Confucius and many since him have wisely said, our character is formed in our thought life: "Sow a thought, reap an action; sow an action; reap a habit; sow a habit, reap a character; sow a character, reap a destiny." God wants us to dwell on what is true, noble, right, pure, lovely, admirable, excellent, and praiseworthy, and those thoughts will shape our character and our attitude toward life.

It is impossible to control all our thoughts or to block out all negative stimuli. But we do have control over what we allow ourselves to be exposed to habitually (books, friends, media, places, etc.) For example, we can make sure that the primary input for our minds is from the Word of God. If I can cultivate good thoughts and nurture them with good input, I will be more joyful.

10. **Rather than getting bogged down in the difficulties of the present, look at things in the sweep of God's perspective for the future.**

But our citizenship is in heaven. And we eagerly await a Savior from there, the Lord Jesus Christ, who, by the power that enables him to bring everything under his control, will transform our lowly bodies so that they will be like his glorious body (3:20-21).

It's easy to get our thinking locked into our own little niche in space and time. But by faith we can see far beyond the confines of our own physical and temporal limitations. Paul gives us a glimpse into what God's plan holds for the future: the return of our Savior, everything being brought fully under His control, and the transformation of our lowly bodies into glorious bodies. Someday all of our troubles will be behind us. We can look forward to that day with joyful anticipation.

If we walk by sight we will look around and see problems, ugliness, sorrow, and despair. If we walk by faith we will look up and see peace, beauty, joy, and hope. Where do you want to fix your eyes?

Rejoicing is not an option for the Christian; it is a command. Paul says, "Rejoice in the Lord always. I will say it again: Rejoice!" In fact, he speaks of joy or rejoicing at least 14 times in the book of Philippians. Many times the outward circumstances do not warrant rejoicing. It must be an act of faith, rooted in the goodness and sovereignty of God. So what will you choose to do?

complain or be content?

compete or cooperate?

glorify self or glorify God?

wallow in guilt or receive forgiveness?

whine about suffering or rejoice in it?

get angry or intercede?

work *for* your salvation or work *out* your salvation?

worry or pray?

dwell on the negative or dwell on the positive?

walk by sight or walk by faith?

As Paul shows in Philippians, there are many daily choices we can make in order to experience joy. You don't have to wait for happiness to happen to you—you can choose joy today!

TEACHER, TEACHER, MAKE THEM STOP IT!

Mommeee, Ella called me a tattletale!

Really? What on earth made her say such a thing?

The quibbling of my granddaughters makes us smile, but all too often we are just like little children—accusing and tattling on one another. As Mark records, Jesus had to deal with this problem when John complained about someone else who wasn't doing ministry the "right" way:

> John: Teacher, Teacher, we saw someone driving out demons in your name and we told him to stop it because he isn't one of our group.

> Jesus: Don't stop him. No one who does a miracle in my name will turn around the next minute and say something bad about me. Whoever is not against us is on our team. [paraphrase of Mark 9:38-39]

The Apostle Peter, Mark's mentor, also warned about being a busybody and interfering in other people's business: "But let none of you suffer as a murderer or a thief or an evildoer or as a meddler" (1 Pet. 4:15). Meddling is right up there with murder, stealing, and evildoing!

When one of my kids would point the finger at another, I used to tell them, "Never mind about your brother or sister. Just take care of yourself—that's a big enough job." Similarly, Jesus had to tell John to take care of himself and not try to be the policeman of others. God has many people in many places doing His work in many ways. The Lord Himself is able to deal with His other children who may get off track. Our job is to keep our eyes fixed on Him and follow Him in obedience.

This problem is nothing new, but in the digital age the bickering among believers can quickly become very public and very ugly. High-profile accusations by Christians against one another detract from our ministry and leave a stain on our witness. Let us instead love, respect, and serve one another so that the world can say of us what the pagans said of Christians in the third century, "See how they love one another!"

---

[1] Tertullian. Apology 39.7

"I KNOW MY REDEEMER LIVES"

E ven through the great despair that characterizes much of the book of Job, there are echoes of redemption everywhere, the centerpiece being Job's affirmation of his belief in a living Redeemer in 19:25. Job and his friends speak of the longing in the human heart that one day everything will be made right, and the book gives glimpses of hope that it will happen.

Job is a difficult book to interpret not only because some of the language is obscure, but also because the words of all five human speakers—Job, Eliphaz, Bildad, Zophar, and Elihu—contain a mixture of truth and error. It is not easy to sort out the truth from the error, but through reading the book we can discover that we are very much like ancient people, with the same hopes and longings, and that God has been working out His eternal purposes for them and for us since the beginning of time.

At first Job enjoyed a life full of blessings and free from suffering. He was extremely prosperous, he had a great family and many friends, he was respected in the community, and his relationship with God was good. But when everything was stripped away from him, he became acutely and very personally aware that something is desperately wrong with the world. He wished he had died at birth rather than live to suffer: "Why did I not perish at birth, and die as I came from the womb?" (3:11).

Job wondered "why is light given to those in misery, and life to the bitter of soul, to those who long for death that does not come, who search for it more than for hidden treasure, who are filled with gladness and rejoice when they reach the grave?" (3:20-22). Death would be a welcome relief—to go to the place where no one suffers:

> For now I would be lying down in peace;
>> I would be asleep and at rest
> with kings and counselors of the earth,
>> who built for themselves places now lying in ruins,
> with rulers who had gold,
>> who filled their houses with silver.
> Or why was I not hidden in the ground like a stillborn child,
>> like an infant who never saw the light of day?
> There the wicked cease from turmoil,
>> and there the weary are at rest.
> Captives also enjoy their ease;
>> they no longer hear the slave driver's shout.
> The small and the great are there,
>> and the slave is freed from his master (3:13-19).

Yet despite Job's desire that it would all just be over so he would be released from his misery, he sensed that there had to be more—that there *must* be a way to be restored and renewed and reconciled to God. Recognizing that he could not defend himself to an infinite God, Job expressed his need for a mediator—someone to represent him before God:

> He is not a man like me that I might answer him,
>> that we might confront each other in court.
> If only there were someone to arbitrate between us,
>> to lay his hand upon us both.
> someone to remove God's rod from me,
>> so that his terror would frighten me no more
>> (9:32-34).

> Even now my witness is in heaven;
>> my advocate is on high.
> My intercessor is my friend
>> as my eyes pour out tears to God;

on behalf of a man he pleads with God
as a man pleads for his friend (16:19-21).

Job didn't know who the mediator/redeemer/arbitrator/
witness/advocate/intercessor/friend might be, but we know
that He is Jesus, whose suffering ransomed us from death:

For there is one God and one mediator between God
and mankind, the man Christ Jesus, who gave himself
as a ransom for all people (1 Timothy 2:5-6).

Job also glimpsed the promise that God has more in store
for us beyond this life:

Though he slay me, yet will I hope in him;... Indeed,
this will turn out for my deliverance (13:15-16).

If a man dies, will he live again?
All the days of my hard service
I will wait for my renewal to come.
You will call and I will answer you;
you will long for the creature
your hands have made (14:14-15).

And ultimately he declares his belief in a living Redeemer
who will come to restore him:

I know that my Redeemer lives,
and that in the end he will stand upon the earth.
And after my skin has been destroyed,
yet in my flesh I will see God;
I myself will see him
with my own eyes—I, and not another.
How my heart yearns within me! (19:25-27)

When God confronted Job at the end of the book, Job
realized how insignificant he was before the Creator, and yet,
this God reaches down to enter into an intimate relationship
with human beings. As Nicole Mullen's song "I Know My
Redeemer Lives" expresses it, "The very same God that spins
things in orbit / Runs to the weary, the worn, and the weak."

Who taught the sun where to stand in the morning?
And who told the ocean you can only come this far?
And who showed the moon where to hide till evening?
Whose words alone can catch a falling star?

The very same God that spins things in orbit
Runs to the weary, the worn and the weak
And the same gentle hands that hold me when I'm
    broken
They conquered death to bring me victory.

Well I know my Redeemer lives
I know my Redeemer lives
All of creation testifies
This life within me cries
I know my Redeemer lives![1]

Redemption is a powerful theme that runs throughout
Scripture, from the moment it first became necessary, in
Genesis 3, through the final words of Revelation. Right after
the fall, God hinted to Adam and Eve that the offspring of
the woman would crush the head of Satan, the one who
drives the wedge between God and man. In Job, Satan challenged God and lost—a foretaste of his final defeat. As Job
affirmed, "I know that you can do all things; no plan of yours
can be thwarted" (42:2). God not only defeated Satan but also
redeemed the suffering of Job and blessed him mightily in the
end: "The Lord blessed the latter part of Job's life more than
the first" (42:12). Job was a living demonstration of how God
brings new life out of ashes and restores His creation to what
it was intended to be.

God put in our hearts the understanding that something
is terribly wrong with the world and the longing for everything to be made right, and He will not leave that longing
unfulfilled. Throughout history God has been in the business
of redeeming this lost and fallen world and blessing His
children, and one day He will fully accomplish the reversal of
the curse and the healing of the nations:

Then the angel showed me the river of the water of life, as clear as crystal, flowing from the throne of God and of the Lamb down the middle of the great street of the city. On each side of the river stood the tree of life, bearing twelve crops of fruit, yielding its fruit every month. And the leaves of the tree are for the healing of the nations. No longer will there be any curse (Rev. 22:1-3).

Like Job's restoration to double his fortune and family, God will so completely overturn Satan's plans for destruction that the final outcome will be more glorious than if sin and suffering had never happened. The Holy One of Israel is our Redeemer (Is. 54:5). Our Redeemer lives and reigns! And He will raise us up to live and reign with Him!

---

[1] "I Know My Redeemer Lives," by Nicole Mullen, 2000.

THE VEIL TALE

Time and again the Lord gives us special gifts of providence that remind us of His ceaseless care over us. These are not the spectacular miracles that He also does from time to time, but rather His providential workings through the ordinary circumstances of life, whispering of His constant presence and His gracious kindness. We experienced one of these delightful conjunctions of events on the occasion of my daughter's wedding. The tale of the veil is a story that will go down in the lore of her wedding.

Having hit horrendous traffic going into the city Friday night for the rehearsal, we left in plenty of time Saturday afternoon for the 3:00 wedding. We did have a scare Saturday morning when we got word that our 7-year-old granddaughter Emmy had thrown up everywhere. She had also had to go to the hospital the day before for a little surgery to cut a piece of pencil lead out of her leg—the result of an accidental stabbing with a pencil while playing at school. We were particularly nervous because her mom was an attendant in the wedding, but by early afternoon Emmy was doing better and they were also on their way. She had a bucket in hand but never needed to use it. It seemed that everything was on track.

Then at 1:45 the bride called me in alarm to see if anyone was still at home to bring her veil, which she had left at our house months ago. But everybody was already on the road and if anyone had turned back they would have been late for the wedding, which would have been worse than not having the veil. My heart sank at my own stupidity for not bringing it, and Michelle resigned herself to not having it. But without telling Michelle I got on the phone and called the home of some friends. I explained the situation, and their son David said, "I'm on it."

Fortunately I had left a key in the recycle bin outside for the friend who was coming to walk the dogs, so there was a way for David to get into the house. I told him where the key was, and I gave him the address of the church to plug into his GPS, but I found out later that he didn't have a GPS! He knew the general direction of where to go, but the church was not easy to get to. When he got close he saw a cab driver—an angel in disguise in answer to prayer! The cab was stopped at an intersection, and David was able to pull up beside it and ask for directions. The cabby said to go left and then left again and he'd be there.

Meanwhile, we were at the church waiting for the limo bringing the wedding party. I was holding my phone on vibrate waiting for a call from Dave. Finally everyone was assembled, but no veil. When it was my turn to go down the aisle, I handed my phone off to my son Daniel and told him to go outside and be watching for Dave. I figured that Michelle would at least have the veil for her pictures afterward.

All eyes were on the attendants as they came down the aisle after me, and then on the darling ring bearer and flower girl with their banners: "Here comes the bride" / "and the groom." Then I looked to the back of the church where Michelle was starting down the aisle. Beside her head above her shoulders I saw sheer white triangles. I thought my eyes were playing tricks—it must be the light! I didn't dare believe it was the veil until she was close enough for me to really see it! Then she passed me and I saw the whole thing flowing down her back over her beautiful hair, and my eyes filled with tears. I learned afterward that David had pulled up just in the nick of time and passed the veil off to Dan, who brought it to Michelle. Truly, getting it at the last minute unexpectedly was better than if everything had gone smoothly in the first place! And an added special touch was that the one who saved the day was David, the son of our friend Eric. The groom had lost his older brother Eric when they were teenagers, and even in the joy of the wedding day, there was sadness that Eric was not with us. Having the son of an Eric bring the veil made the memory of Adam's brother Eric even stronger and more present.

May the Veil Tale be a reminder of the daily blessings from the hand of our good God!

The steadfast love of the Lord never ceases;
    his mercies never come to an end;
they are new every morning;
    great is your faithfulness.
Lamentations 3:22-23

UNITY IN DIVERSITY
AND DISAGREEMENT

R omans 14 talks about how to get along with other Christians who may be very different from ourselves. This is a challenge I have encountered every day for more than 40 years because my husband, Tony, is Peruvian.

Let me tell you a little about Latin Americans. Latinos love to party for any occasion, and their idea of what makes a great party might be quite different from ours. Listen to a teacher from a Costa Rican elementary school as she describes a Mother's Day open house at the school, as quoted in the book *From the Other's Point of View:*[1]

> The Mother's Day party—what a beautiful occasion. School was crowded from 8 till 2. Everybody was there. Mothers smiling. Children proud of their mothers. Programs. Banners. Food. The dances and the flowers. Do you know that the third grade put on a play, and the fifth grade actually hired a combo? The whole thing—beautiful!

How different her perception from that of a North American mother whose daughter attended the school! To read her account, you wonder if they were describing the same event:

> In all my life, I've never seen such bedlam. And spare me of it again. Mass confusion, swarms of people, yelling and screaming, horns and drums. I tried to find Kathy's classroom, and frankly it was a case of total chaos. Even the teacher didn't seem to know what was going on. There was to be a play, yet nobody knew

what the play was to be. The kids did put something on, but I heard nothing of it thanks to roving troubadours outside. Mothers shouted "Louder! Louder!" but we heard nothing. What was the point of the party?

Sometimes the task of getting along with others despite our differences simply requires good-natured acceptance and a sense of humor. But often our differences strike deeper at the heart of who we are and what we value. See the shock of Bill, an American exchange student, over the treatment of handicapped people that he observed in Costa Rica:

> The people of this nation are cruel to handicapped persons. In my year here, I've seen grown men teasing a mentally retarded boy. I've seen boys pitching pebbles at an old man. Even in private homes, I've seen grandparents teased. To top it off, last week at the immigration office a lad went to a window and asked what time the office would close. A bad speech impediment forced him to use *l* instead of *r*. The clerk responded loudly, mocking the impediment by using an *l* for each *r* in her answer. The office staff laughed.

But his Costa Rican friend Carlos saw the situation in a totally different light:

> Bill sees and hears teasing, but he misunderstands it. We tease everyone here. Everyone whom we like. To be teased is to be a part of the family. We keep handicapped people in our homes and treat them like anyone else. Sure, we tease them in any way we can. In the United States, you put handicapped and elderly people away in institutions where you don't talk at all with them. That is what I would call cruelty.

So who is right? Don't we all have a tendency to assume that *our* way of looking at things is the *right* way, that our sense of morality is correct? In some cultures it is acceptable for women to go bare-breasted but considered indecent to show their legs. Do we react by thinking, "How backward"?

We don't have to cross foreign borders to find profound differences between people. Even among Christians, who have in common the value system of the Bible, there are still different ways of looking at things. In our churches and in our personal relationships, we need tools to deal with these differences constructively.

The early church faced this same dilemma—how to bring together in one body a very diverse group of people, all united by their common faith in Christ but separated by different cultures, backgrounds, perceptions, and levels of maturity. In chapter 14 of Romans, Paul uses a problem in the Roman church to illustrate how we can deal with the differences that tend to divide us.

We're not talking here about theological or moral truths— the essential elements of our faith or the absolute commands of Scripture. For example, the resurrection is the cornerstone of our faith, and the Ten Commandments provide the moral base. The Bible makes it clear that certain beliefs and actions are right and others are wrong, and when something is specifically taught or commanded in Scripture, we need look no further in order to know what is right. But here we are talking about the vast gray area between the black and the white— the non-essentials, the peripherals outside the core values, the issues where the Bible is silent or allows some degree of latitude. Paul gives us principles to guide us in the gray area—to help us make good decisions as well as to be gracious toward others as they make choices that differ from ours.

The specific issue confronting the early church is not one that we face today, but it is representative of the kinds of questions we must wrestle with, and the principles Paul teaches can be applied to any situation.

It was customary in the ancient world to kill animals as sacrifices to pagan gods and then sell the leftover meat for food. Some of the Roman Christians wanted no part of anything even remotely connected to pagan worship, and they refused to buy or eat this meat. We might think of them as the strong ones, who had the willpower to resist anything that might be questionable, but Paul referred to them as "weak" Christians, not because they were morally weak but because they were afraid that by eating this food they were participating in pagan worship and their faith could be undermined. As a contemporary example, when we were first married, someone gave us three bottles of wine. As a young Christian I was so nervous about having alcohol in the house that I dumped it out. I was weak then, but now my faith is more mature and I could accept the gift graciously.

Others of the Roman Christians, realizing that idols are nothing, knew that meat offered to idols was not "contaminated," and they could eat it in good conscience. Paul says that they are the "strong" ones because their faith is solid enough not to be shaken by eating this food.

When we go to the meat counter at the grocery store, we don't pause to wonder whether the meat has been offered to idols. But we do face similar dilemmas. One that comes around every year is what to do about Halloween. Some Christians want nothing to do with this holiday that has pagan roots and satanic overtones. Others feel they can participate in the fun aspects of the holiday without promoting those elements that are anti-Christian. A good case can be made for both sides, with many factors affecting each individual's viewpoint, and we should respect each other's decisions.

In our everyday lives we encounter many situations where true Christians have legitimate differences about what to believe or how to act—outworking of husband-wife roles, career choices, birth control and family size, childrearing, how to educate our kids and where, spending and giving habits, politics, music, the media, alcohol, speaking in tongues and other spiritual gifts, ways of observing the Lord's Day or Christmas or Easter—the list is endless. If you struggle with issues of this sort or find yourself disagreeing with other Christians regarding these touchy matters, Romans 14 can help.

First of all, Paul says to **accept each other**—to recognize each other as genuine Christians and to welcome each other in the body. The people with whom we have these sincere disagreements are not heretics but brothers and sisters in Christ. Verse 3 says that God accepts them as His children—we have no right not to recognize them as such. We are not to allow our differences to create discord within the church. This point is crucial because the way we relate in the body is a reflection on the Head. In verse 7 of chapter 15 Paul says, "Accept one another, then, just as Christ accepted you, in order to bring praise to God." Our ultimate purpose in all we do is to glorify God. By embracing all believers with acceptance and love, we promote unity within the church, which in turn brings glory to God.

In the second part of verse one, Paul says **do not pass judgment on disputable matters**—in other words, do not make absolute pronouncements of right and wrong in matters where the Bible allows for a variety of responses. As the Living Bible puts it, "Do not criticize [a brother] for having different ideas from yours about what is right and wrong." Years ago I heard a statement that really stuck with me. It was a two-part statement. First, Satan deceives unbelievers by turning absolutes into relatives. The world says that to stand on the absolutes of the Bible is narrow-minded. They take God's absolute truths and standards and make them optional. With this scheme Satan has done a magnificent job of striking down God's truth and His laws.

But it was the second part of the statement that really caught my attention. He said that Satan deceives Christians by turning relatives into absolutes. In other words, we let human traditions or personal preferences set the standards of right and wrong. We make rules that go beyond what the Bible teaches and say that all Christians should follow them. We think we know what other Christians ought to do. How effective this strategy of Satan has been! It causes us to lose our focus on what is really important as we major on the minors. It creates a rigidity and lack of vitality in the church as we try to squeeze everyone into the same mold. In 1 Corinthians 4:6, Paul warns that going "beyond what is written"—that is, imposing standards that Scripture does not

83

impose—causes "pride in one man over against another." Pride in turn results in division, dysfunction, and disunity within the body. We need to be careful never to waver from God's standards of right and wrong, yet at the same time, to allow as much latitude for Christian freedom as God does.

A third principle is found in verses 3 and 4 and reiterated in verses 10 and 13: **do not judge others**. The "strong" should not look down on those who have super-sensitive scruples, and the "weak" should not condemn those who do things that they deem unfitting, but rather we should all respect the choices of others. God leads different people in different ways, and we should not presume to know what He ought to do in other people's lives or what the condition of their heart is.

An incident that happened many years ago taught me a lesson in not judging others. I was in the supermarket one afternoon, and it was terribly crowded. As I made my way toward the checkout, a lady was coming toward me, pushing her carriage. She had bulgy eyes and a red, mean-looking face. Suddenly she crashed her cart right into another lady's cart. The thought went through my mind, "How rude to bump into someone else just to get a place in line!" A second later I felt awful. She apologized profusely to the other woman— "Oh, I'm *so* sorry. I just had an operation on my eyes, and I can't see very well," which explained why she ran into the other cart and also why her eyes were bulgy. I thought I could look inside her and size her up, but I was wrong.

In verse 5 and again in verse 23, we see how important it is to **follow our conscience**. Paul says, "Each one should be fully convinced in his own mind." While I should not let my personal convictions dictate what someone *else* ought to do, I should be careful not to violate my own conscience in what *I* do. Paul says that "if anyone regards something as unclean, then for *him* it *is* unclean" (14:14), and therefore wrong for him. If I go ahead and do something that my conscience tells me not to do, even though another good Christian says it's fine, my conscience is dulled a bit and I lose some of my sensitivity to right and wrong. If I go against my conscience in one thing, it becomes a little easier to go against it in another. But if I make it a practice to fill my mind with the Word of God and then listen to my sanctified conscience, I will grow in discernment and be better able to perceive what God wants me to do.

In verses 6-8, the phrase "to the Lord" or "to God" appears eight times. We are to **live to the Lord**. *He* should be the focus and the reason for all that we do. As 1 Corinthians 10:31 says, "Whether you eat or drink or whatever you do, do it all for the glory of God." Have you ever found yourself in a situation where you felt torn trying to please others? Maybe your mother wanted you to do one thing, your mother-in-law thought you should do something else, your neighbor had his ideas, and people at church had different opinions. You may have thought, "I wish I had to please only *one* person!" There *is* only one Person I have to please; God is the Judge to whom I am accountable and whose opinion really matters. Knowing that He is the one I have to please frees me from the stress of being pulled in different directions, and it releases me from the impossible bind of trying to please everyone.

Doing everything unto the Lord knowing that we must give an account to God also means that we **let God do His work in His way in others' lives**. As The Message puts it in verse 12, "So tend to your knitting. You've got your hands full just taking care of your own life before God." Jesus had to tell Peter the same thing. After His resurrection, Jesus met with His disciples on the shores of Galilee. There He gave Peter a glimpse into what lay in store for him in the future. Peter turned around and saw John and asked, "Lord, what about *him*?" Jesus answered, "If I want him to remain alive until I return, what is that to you? You must follow me." We too need to **follow Jesus and keep our eyes fixed on Him**.

Finally, Paul says we should never do anything that might trip up another believer; rather we should **make every effort to do what leads to peace and mutual edification** (v. 19).

Do not cause anyone to stumble; "it is better not to eat meat or drink wine or to do anything else that will cause your brother to fall" (v. 21). After all, Christ *died* for that brother or sister (v. 15); certainly I can modify what I do out of concern for him or her.

I would venture to say that most of the decisions we make in the course of a day or a week or a lifetime are of the gray-area variety. Sometimes I wish that the Bible came in a 50-volume set with a verse for every occasion. If such a thing did exist, I'm sure that by now someone would have invented a computer program so you could just plug in the data for your situation and out would pop a chapter and verse telling you exactly what to do. But that would eliminate the need to get to *know God*. Our relationship with Him is not to be mechanical or to consist of a list of do's and don'ts, but rather the written Word is to lead us directly to the living incarnate Word. He wants us to spend time with Him, to try to understand His mind, to obey the general principles given in His Word, and to seek Him out personally for the specifics in our lives. As The Message puts it in verse 22, "Cultivate your own relationship with God, but don't impose it on others." The Lord wants to see His body, the Church, living together in harmony, united in the essentials but free to flower with all its magnificent diversity. We need to ask God to help us be solid as a rock when it comes to the essentials of our Christian faith and morals, but tolerant of legitimate differences in the non-essentials, with the wisdom to know which are which and love to cover all.

Let us make Paul's prayer in Romans 15:5-6 our prayer:

O God, who gives endurance and encouragement,
give us a spirit of unity among ourselves as we
follow Christ Jesus, so that with one heart and mouth
we may glorify the God and Father of our Lord Jesus Christ.

---

[1] Hess, J. Daniel. *From the Other's Point of View*, 1999

ALWAYS BE READY
TO GIVE THE REASON FOR YOUR HOPE

The *Autobiography of Mark Twain,* the first volume of which was published in 2010 on the one-hundredth anniversary of his death, is a collection of anecdotes, reminiscences, and essays about a vast range of topics from the fertile mind of one of America's beloved authors. The recently published second volume reveals more about his life and thoughts, with his characteristic humor, inquisitiveness, and incisiveness.

In the entry for June 19, 1906 in Volume 2, the author gives his thoughts about the character of the God of the Bible. It quickly becomes apparent that Mark Twain has little use for this God:

> In the old Testament His acts expose His vindictive, unjust, ungenerous, pitiless and vengeful nature constantly. He is always punishing—punishing trifling misdeeds with thousand-fold severity; punishing innocent children for the misdeeds of their parents; punishing unoffending populations for the misdeeds of their rulers; even descending to wreak bloody vengeance upon harmless calves and lambs and sheep and bullocks, as punishment for inconsequential trespasses committed by their proprietors.

His words bring to mind the tirade of atheist Richard Dawkins in his book *The God Delusion:*

The God of the Old Testament is arguably the most unpleasant character in all fiction: jealous and proud of it; a petty, unjust, unforgiving control-freak; a vindictive, bloodthirsty ethnic cleanser; a misogynistic, homophobic, racist, infanticidal, genocidal, filicidal, pestilential, megalomaniacal, sadomasochistic, capriciously malevolent bully.

Peter says that we should "always be prepared to give an answer to everyone who asks you to give the reason for the hope that you have" (1 Pet. 3:15). How could we share our hope with people like Mark Twain and his contemporary counterparts like Richard Dawkins, Daniel Dennett, and Sam Harris? I encourage you to read Mark Twain's words thoughtfully and think about how you could share the gospel with someone like him. If we are prepared, God may bring such people across our path and give us opportunity to reach out to them. But as Peter cautions, "do this with gentleness and respect, keeping a clear conscience, so that those who speak maliciously against your good behavior [or against God's character] may be ashamed of their slander" (1 Pet. 3:16).

Here are some more principles to keep in mind as we share our faith with people who scoff at the God of the Bible:

Let your conversation be always full of grace, seasoned with salt, so that you may know how to answer everyone (Col. 4:6).

Opponents must be gently instructed, in the hope that God will grant them repentance leading them to a knowledge of the truth (2 Tim. 2:25).

Through thick and thin, keep your hearts at attention, in adoration before Christ, your Master. Be ready to speak up and tell anyone who asks why you're living the way you are, and always with the utmost courtesy. Keep a clear conscience before God so that when people throw mud at you, none of it will stick (1 Pet. 3:15-16, *The Message*).

RULES FOR EFFECTIVE LEADERSHIP

B eing in the corporate world gave me an opportunity to compare and contrast leadership styles. Worldly leaders who want to lord it over others might follow these "rules," but let it not be so among Christian leaders!

1) **Don't bother to learn people's names.** You have weightier matters to think about—you shouldn't have to clutter your mind with details like people's names. They don't care anyway.

2) **Don't mingle with the commoners.** You are too important to be spending your time with ordinary people. If you want to be the big cheese, you have to maintain distance between yourself and your subordinates. Make them think you always have it together; never reveal your own weaknesses, fears, and failures.

3) **Don't listen to their sob stories.** Let them know that you are too busy to hear about their problems and woes.

4) **Don't provide job descriptions or divulge your expectations.** If people want to know what they are supposed to do, they ought to figure it out themselves. Keep them guessing, and you will stay in control.

5) **Don't give any positive feedback.** If you encourage people, it will just go to their heads, so keep quiet if they happen to do something right. However, if they mess up, be sure to let them know right away. Telling others about someone's failings will also help keep that person in line.

6) **Keep people from connecting with each other.** By associating with others, they might be strengthened and become a threat to your leadership.

7) **Make decisions unilaterally.** It is too time-consuming and tedious to get into discussions with other people. You are perfectly capable of evaluating a situation and figuring out what needs to be done, so just decide what you want to do and proceed to do it.

8) **Don't be accountable to anyone else.** Make sure no one is looking over your shoulder—you don't want anyone exposing problems in your life.

9) **Keep your subjects' noses to the grindstone.** If you allow them to have fun, they will be wasting time that could be spent doing something productive.

10) **If you pass someone, don't make eye contact or acknowledge the person.** Keep an aloof demeanor so they know how important you are. Be sure not to smile.

But Jesus called them to him and said, "You know that the rulers of the Gentiles lord it over them, and their great ones exercise authority over them. It shall not be so among you. But whoever would be great among you must be your **servant**, and whoever would be first among you must be your slave, even as the Son of Man came not to be served but to serve, and to give his life as a ransom for many" (Mt. 20:25-28).

DOES GOD'S WILL TRUMP MAN'S FREE WILL? PART 1

S omeone once accused me of believing that "God's will trumps man's free will." I happily plead guilty as charged. God is sovereign almost by definition, and I have never questioned the fact that God created and rules the universe. But the discussion got me thinking about what the Bible actually says about God's sovereignty and what exactly it means. I started looking for passages that speak to this question, and the evidence is overwhelming that God's will does indeed trump man's free will.

From Genesis to Revelation, the sovereignty of God is affirmed. *Nave's Topical Bible* helped me find passages about God's sovereignty in every section of the Bible.

Throughout the **Pentateuch** (the first five books of the Bible), starting with the opening verse of Genesis, the Lord is declared to be the Creator and Ruler of the universe:

In the beginning, God created the heavens and the earth (Gen. 1:1).

God Most High, Possessor of heaven and earth (Gen. 14:19, 22).

The LORD, the God of heaven and God of the earth (Gen. 24:3).

The earth is the LORD's (Ex. 9:29).

The LORD will reign forever and ever (Ex. 15:18).

The LORD is God in heaven above and on the earth beneath; there is no other (Deut. 4:39).

For the LORD your God is God of gods and Lord of lords, the great, the mighty, and the awesome God (Deut. 10:17).

See now that I, even I, am he,
      and there is no god beside me;
I kill and I make alive;
      I wound and I heal;
      and there is none that can deliver out of my hand
      (Deut. 32:39).

The **historical books** show God fulfilling His own purposes on earth despite the rebellion of men. Even Ruth, the book that does not mention the name of God, shows how He works sovereignly in the affairs of men to accomplish His will.

The LORD your God, he is God in the heavens above and on the earth beneath (Josh. 2:11).

The LORD kills and brings to life;
      he brings down to Sheol and raises up.
The LORD makes poor and makes rich;
      he brings low and he exalts.
He raises up the poor from the dust;
      he lifts the needy from the ash heap
to make them sit with princes
      and inherit a seat of honor.
For the pillars of the earth are the LORD's,
      and on them he has set the world (1 Sam. 2:6-8).

You are the God, you alone, of all the kingdoms of the earth; you have made heaven and earth (2 Ki. 19:15).

Yours, O LORD, is the greatness and the power and the glory and the victory and the majesty, for all that is in the heavens and in the earth is yours. Yours is the kingdom, O LORD, and you are exalted as head above all. Both riches and honor come from you, and you rule over all. In your hand are power and might, and in your hand it is to make great and to give strength to all (1 Chr. 29:11-12).

O LORD, God of our fathers, are you not God in heaven? You rule over all the kingdoms of the nations. In your hand are power and might, so that none is able to withstand you (2 Chr. 20:6).

You are the LORD, you alone. You have made heaven, the heaven of heavens, with all their host, the earth and all that is on it, the seas and all that is in them; and you preserve all of them; and the host of heaven worships you (Neh. 9:6).

The foundation of the **wisdom literature** is that the fear of God is the beginning of wisdom. The writers knew full well that God is the source, sustainer, and ruler of all. The Psalms are especially rich with bold declarations of God's sovereignty.

In his hand is the life of every living thing
and the breath of all mankind (Job 12:10).

But he is unchangeable, and who can turn him back?
What he desires, that he does (Job 23:13).

Who has first given to me, that I should repay him?
Whatever is under the whole heaven is mine
(Job 41:11).

I know that you can do all things,
and that no purpose of yours can be thwarted
(Job 42:2).

For kingship belongs to the Lord,
and he rules over the nations (Ps. 22:28)

The LORD sits enthroned as king forever (Ps. 29:10).

For he spoke, and it came to be;
he commanded, and it stood firm....

The LORD brings the counsel of the nations to
nothing;
he frustrates the plans of the peoples.
The counsel of the LORD stands forever,
the plans of his heart to all generations
(Ps. 33:9-11).

God reigns over the nations;
God sits on his holy throne (Ps. 47:8).

You alone, whose name is the LORD,
are the Most High over all the earth (Ps. 83:18).

The heavens are yours; the earth also is yours;
the world and all that is in it, you have founded
them (Ps. 89:11).

For you, O LORD, are most high over all the earth;
you are exalted far above all gods (Ps. 97:9).

The LORD has established his throne in the heavens,
and his kingdom rules over all (Ps. 103:19).

The LORD is high above all nations,
and his glory above the heavens! (Ps. 113:4).

Our God is in the heavens; he does all that he pleases
(Ps. 115:3).

For I know that the LORD is great,
and that our Lord is above all gods.
Whatever the LORD pleases, he does,
in heaven and on earth,
in the seas and all deeps (Ps. 135:5-6).

Your kingdom is an everlasting kingdom,
and your dominion endures throughout all
generations (Ps. 145:13).

No wisdom, no understanding, no counsel
can avail against the LORD (Prov. 21:30).

But all this I laid to heart, examining it all, how the righteous and the wise and their deeds are in the hand of God (Eccl. 9:1).

Part 2 will show God's sovereignty in the prophets, the gospels, Acts, the epistles, and Revelation.

DOES GOD'S WILL TRUMP MAN'S FREE WILL? PART 2

P art 1 showed God's sovereignty in the Pentateuch, the historical books, and the wisdom literature. If any doubt remains, consider the evidence in the prophets and the whole New Testament.

The **prophets** exalt the name of God and affirm that His purposes will stand.

> The LORD of hosts has sworn:
> "As I have planned,
>   so shall it be,
> and as I have purposed,
>   so shall it stand....
> This is the purpose that is purposed
>   concerning the whole earth,
> and this is the hand that is stretched out
>   over all the nations.
> For the LORD of hosts has purposed,
>   and who will annul it?
> His hand is stretched out,
>   and who will turn it back? (Isa. 14:24-27).

> O LORD of hosts, enthroned above the cherubim, you are the God, you alone, of all the kingdoms of the earth; you have made heaven and earth (Is. 37:16).

> It is he who sits above the circle of the earth;
>   its inhabitants are like grasshoppers (Isa. 40:22).

Thus says God, the LORD,
> who created the heavens and stretched them out,
> who spread out the earth and what comes from it,
who gives breath to the people on it
> and spirit to those who walk in it (Isa. 42:5).

Thus says the LORD, the King of Israel
> and his Redeemer, the LORD of hosts:
"I am the first and I am the last;
> besides me there is no god (Isa. 44:6).

By myself I have sworn;
> from my mouth has gone out in righteousness
> a word that shall not return:
"To me every knee shall bow,
> every tongue shall swear allegiance" (Isa. 45:23).

"I am God, and there is no other;
> I am God, and there is none like me,
declaring the end from the beginning
> and from ancient times things not yet done,
saying, 'My counsel shall stand,
> and I will accomplish all my purpose,'...
I have spoken, and I will bring it to pass;
> I have purposed, and I will do it." (Is. 46:9-11).

Ah, Lord GOD! It is you who have made the heavens and the earth by your great power and by your outstretched arm! Nothing is too hard for you (Jer. 32:17).

"Behold, I am the LORD, the God of all flesh. Is anything too hard for me? (Jer. 32:27).

But you, O LORD, reign forever;
> your throne endures to all generations
> (Lam. 5:19).

I am the LORD; I have spoken, and I will do it (Ez. 17:24).

Blessed be the name of God forever and ever,
    to whom belong wisdom and might.
    He changes times and seasons;
    he removes kings and sets up kings;
he gives wisdom to the wise
    and knowledge to those who have understanding;
    he reveals deep and hidden things;
    he knows what is in the darkness,
    and the light dwells with him (Dan. 2:21-22).

His kingdom is an everlasting kingdom,
    and his dominion endures from generation to
    generation (Dan 4:3).

The Most High rules the kingdom of men and gives it
to whom he will (Dan. 4:25).

All the inhabitants of the earth are accounted as nothing, and He does according to His will among the host of heaven and among the inhabitants of the earth; and none can stay His hand or say to Him, "What have you done?" (Dan. 4:35)

All his works are right and his ways are just; and those who walk in pride he is able to humble (Dan. 4:37).

The New Testament reinforces everything the Old Testament says about the power of God. In the **gospels**, Jesus teaches about the sovereignty of God and how He and His Father work together to bring about the Father's will.

Your kingdom come,
your will be done,
    on earth as it is in heaven (Mt. 6:10).

In that same hour he rejoiced in the Holy Spirit and said, "I thank you, Father, Lord of heaven and earth, that you have hidden these things from the wise and understanding and revealed them to little children; yes, Father, for such was your gracious will. All things have been handed over to me by my Father, and no one knows who the Son is except the Father, or who the Father is except the Son and anyone to whom the Son chooses to reveal him" (Lk. 10:21-22).

My Father, who has given them to me, is greater than all, and no one is able to snatch them out of the Father's hand (Jn. 10:29).

The book of **Acts** and the **epistles** recognize God as the sovereign and omnipotent Lord who works everything according to the counsel of His own will.

The God who made the world and everything in it, being Lord of heaven and earth, does not live in temples made by man, nor is he served by human hands, as though he needed anything, since he himself gives to all mankind life and breath and everything. And he made from one man every nation of mankind to live on all the face of the earth, having determined allotted periods and the boundaries of their dwelling place (Acts 17:24-26).

What shall we say then? Is there injustice on God's part? By no means! For he says to Moses, "I will have mercy on whom I have mercy, and I will have compassion on whom I have compassion." So then it depends not on human will or exertion, but on God, who has mercy (Rom. 9:14-16).

Oh, the depth of the riches and wisdom and knowledge of God! How unsearchable are his judgments and how inscrutable his ways! (Rom. 11:33).

As I live, says the Lord, every knee shall bow to me, and every tongue shall confess to God (Rom. 14:11).

For us there is one God, the Father, from whom are all things and for whom we exist, and one Lord, Jesus Christ, through whom are all things and through whom we exist (1 Cor. 8:6).

He works all things according to the counsel of His will (Eph. 1:11).

There is one God and Father of all, who is over all and through all and in all (Eph. 4:6).

By him all things were created, in heaven and on earth, visible and invisible, whether thrones or dominions or rulers or authorities—all things were created through him and for him (Col. 1:16).

He is "the blessed and only Sovereign, the King of kings and Lord of lords" (1 Tim. 6:15).

He is the radiance of the glory of God and the exact imprint of his nature, and he upholds the universe by the word of his power (Heb. 1:3).

And finally, **Revelation** declares that God is the beginning and the end, the Almighty who reigns forever.

"I am the Alpha and the Omega," says the Lord God, "who is and who was and who is to come, the Almighty" (Rev. 1:8).

Worthy are you, our Lord and God,
    to receive glory and honor and power,
for you created all things,
    and by your will they existed and were created
    (Rev. 4:11).

Hallelujah!
For the Lord our God the Almighty reigns (Rev. 19:6).

I am the Alpha and the Omega, the beginning and the end (Rev. 21:6).

I am the Alpha and the Omega, the first and the last, the beginning and the end (Rev. 22:13).

After doing this search, I came away more convinced than ever that God is truly sovereign. Believing that God's will trumps man's free will does not mean that we are robots with absolutely no freedom of choice; we make real choices with real consequences. And often God allows us to act in a way that violates His perfect will. But in the final analysis, no man can thwart God's purposes forever.

(All quotations are from the English Standard Version, ESV.)

ARE YOU FREE?

The Apostle Peter graphically describes the corrupt character of false teachers and sternly warns about the destructive effects of their life and teaching. One way they deceive is by promising freedom while in reality causing people to be entrapped:

> They promise them freedom, but they themselves are slaves of corruption. For whatever overcomes a person, to that he is enslaved (2 Peter 2:19).

As I read those words about being a slave, I thought of friends who are smokers. Yes, they are free to smoke, but they are *not* free *not* to smoke. The smoking slavemaster can interrupt what they are doing at any moment and force them to put a cigarette between their lips. At the office, it drives them outside in the dead of winter just for that precious drag. It holds them in its grip and doesn't let go unless met with a stronger power. Willpower alone is seldom enough; as one friend put it, "It's easy to quit; I've done it a hundred times."

Being "free" to smoke is just an illusion. *Real* freedom is being free *not* to smoke. In a similar way, many are attracted by the lure of throwing off restraints and engaging in sins that seem appealing. It feels like freedom to be able to do anything you want. But eventually you become entrapped to the point where you cannot escape; you have lost the freedom *not* to sin, and you become what Jesus calls "a slave to sin."

A friend was telling me about his cousin, who was a talented surgeon. He turned to drugs to cope with the intense pressure of performing life-or-death surgeries day in and day out. He felt he could handle just a little something to sharpen his senses or give him more energy. The drugs seemed to promise more power, but he was overcome by them and became their slave.

Anyone—Christian or not—can become entrapped by sin. For those who do not know Christ, the first step is to realize that what you need is not just willpower to overcome sin—you need forgiveness from sin and new life in Christ. The Holy Spirit is the source of power and freedom—the One who gives strength to say no to sin and to choose what is right (2 Cor. 3:17).

In Romans 6, Paul says that "we should no longer be slaves to sin" because we have been set free from sin. He goes on to say,

> Therefore do not let sin reign in your mortal body so that you obey its evil desires. Do not offer any part of yourself to sin as an instrument of wickedness, but rather offer yourselves to God as those who have been brought from death to life; and offer every part of yourself to him as an instrument of righteousness. For sin shall no longer be your master, because you are not under the law, but under grace (vv. 12-14).

> Don't you know that when you offer yourselves to someone as obedient slaves, you are slaves of the one you obey—whether you are slaves to sin, which leads to death, or to obedience, which leads to righteousness? But thanks be to God that, though you used to be slaves to sin, you have come to obey from your heart the pattern of teaching that has now claimed your allegiance. You have been set free from sin and have become slaves to righteousness (vv. 16-18).

In Romans 7 Paul is honest about the battle between good and evil that goes on in his inner being. But there is hope! The one who rescues him from being a prisoner of sin is Jesus Christ:

Although I want to do good, evil is right there with me. For in my inner being I delight in God's law; but I see another law at work in me, waging war against the law of my mind and making me a prisoner of the law of sin at work within me. What a wretched man I am! Who will rescue me from this body that is subject to death? Thanks be to God, who delivers me through Jesus Christ our Lord! (Rom. 7:21-25).

Jesus is the one who brings freedom for the captives (Isa. 61:1). As John says, "If the Son sets you free, you will be free indeed" (Jn. 8:36). And what is the purpose of this freedom?

You, my brothers and sisters, were called to be free. But do not use your freedom to indulge the flesh; rather, serve one another humbly in love (Gal. 5:13).

Ask yourself, Do you enjoy the freedom *not* to sin? Do you use your freedom to serve one another humbly in love?

> *True freedom is*
> *not the right*
> *to do what's wrong,*
> *but the power*
> *to do what's right.*

ALL SHALL BE WELL

Marathon Monday 2014 was a day of anticipation and hope. A year earlier, the city of Boston was reeling from the terrorist attacks that left four dead and more than 260 injured. Though the evil was great, the good was greater. Many selfless people courageously stepped forward to help the victims right after the bombings, and millions of people worldwide provided support in countless ways in the months following. People were also inspired to reach out and help others with needs of all kinds. For example, my daughter Christine joined many others to do the whole Marathon route carrying 40-pound packs to raise money for veterans.

In tragedy, strangers were united in ways they never could have imagined. Countless stories tell of lives coming together for good. I experienced one of those poignant moments when I walked out onto the field at Fenway Park to the strains of Leonard Cohen's "Hallelujah" with other Marathon volunteers, victims, and first responders in the opening ceremonies of the Red Sox playoff game on October 4, 2013. In a remarkable turn-around, the Red Sox went from last place in the AL East in 2012 to World Series Champions in 2013, giving the city another terrific boost.

The 2014 Boston Marathon brought a record number of runners and spectators for a marvelous day in which the city reclaimed the beauty and camaraderie of this historic event.

Memories of the previous year's tragedy were ever-present and on people's hearts, but it was a day of joy and resilience and redemption. We volunteers on the medals team were moved and honored to be able to give well-deserved medals to the finishers. Many runners ran in honor of the victims, including the youngest one, Martin Richard, age 8. Celeste Corcoran, who lost both legs in the bombing, ran the final stretch on her running blades, accompanied by her sister and her daughter.

It was the thirty-second and final running of Boston for the incredible Team Hoyt, with dad Dick (age 73) pushing son Rick (age 52) in his wheelchair. Another special runner was Tom Feller, whose mom, Debbie, was a high school classmate of mine. On the anniversary of the bombings he ran the whole route dressed as a patriot and carrying two large American flags. He ran again on Marathon Monday, less than

 a week later, to raise money for a school for children with autism. With more than 32,000 runners I knew it would be unlikely for me to see him, but toward the end of my shift I spotted him and was able to snap a picture. And there are countless other stories, both well-known and very private, of how great good arose from horrific evil.

All the feel-good stories in no way erase the pain and loss suffered by so many. But I'm grateful for a glimpse into how God can redeem even the worst evil for His good purposes. Our hope and peace rest "in the knowledge of God and of Jesus our Lord" (2 Pet. 1:2). There are two key qualities that we need to know about God—that He is *good* and that He is *sovereign*. Being assured that He possesses these two attributes gives us confidence that He is both *willing* and *able* to do all that He has guaranteed in "His precious and very great promises" (2 Pet. 1:4).

HUSBANDS LOVE/WIVES SUBMIT

A man is a person who, if a woman says to him, "Never mind. I'll do it myself," lets her.

A woman is a person who, if she says to a man, "Never mind. I'll do it myself," and he lets her, gets mad.

A man is a person who, if a woman says to him, "Never mind. I'll do it myself," and he lets her and she gets mad, says, "Now what are you mad about?"

A woman is a person who, if she says to a man, "Never mind. I'll do it myself," and he lets her and she gets mad and he says, "Now what are you mad about?" says, "If you don't know I'm not going to tell you."   —Katherine S. Beamer

Marriage is challenging! Primarily because both men and women are sinful, but also because we are very different. Men are mystified by women's minds, and women get exasperated with men's behavior. Learning to live together successfully is a life-long process, with daily lessons. One high school student didn't quite get it. His religion teacher read Genesis 2:24, "For this cause shall a man leave his father and mother and cleave to his wife," and asked, "From this Scripture, what do we learn is important in marriage?" The student blurted out, "Cleavage."

Books and sermons on biblical marriage often focus on passages like Ephesians 5, Colossians 3, 1 Peter 3, and Titus 2, which speak specifically of the husband-wife relationship. But *all* of the commands that tell how to treat other people in general apply to husbands and wives in particular. For example, the "one another" passages in the New Testament give extensive instructions on interpersonal relationships.[1] Here are a few of the dozens of one another commands:

Be at peace with one another.
Love one another (at least a dozen times).
Honor one another above yourselves.
Live in harmony with one another.
Serve one another in love.
Bear one another's burdens.
Be patient, bearing with one another in love.
Be kind and compassionate to one another.
Forgive one another.
Submit to one another out of reverence for Christ.
Encourage one another.
Build one another up.
Spur one another on toward love and good deeds.
Confess your sins to one another.
Pray for one another.
Live in harmony with one another.
Clothe yourselves with humility toward one another.

If husbands and wives followed these instructions, there would be no problems in marriages! All of the commands apply equally to men and women. As 1 Thessalonians 5:15 says, "always seek to do good to one another and to everyone." Verse 14 gives some specifics about how to do good to others: "admonish the idle, encourage the fainthearted, help the weak, be patient with them all." Sometimes the wife will be the fainthearted one who needs encouragement. Sometimes the husband will be the weak one who needs help. Either might fall into idleness and need admonishment. We are all in need of patience.

Following the one another commands would be enough to make any relationship healthy, but we must not neglect the passages that deal specifically with the husband-wife relationship. These passages are often cited to show that there is a hierarchical structure in marriage, with the husband as the head and the wife in submission. They have been used to keep women in subjection and allow men to domineer. Sometimes women react against this authoritarianism by rejecting these passages and even abandoning the church altogether.

So what does God want us to learn from His instructions regarding husbands and wives? What does Paul mean when he says in Ephesians 5, "Wives, submit to your own husbands" and "Husbands, love your wives"? We know from earlier in the chapter that *both* husbands and wives are to love one another (v. 2) and *both* are to submit to one another (v. 21), so neither love nor submission is a one-way street.

Paul is saying that both love and submission are to be mutual, and perhaps in verses 22-33 he is not establishing a hierarchy but rather observing human nature and zeroing in on respective weaknesses of men and women. Men seem to have more trouble in the love department. Women tend to be more caring and sacrificial and intuitive by nature, but men are often focused more on themselves. Men know how to love and care for *themselves* but have difficulty putting others' needs first. Therefore Paul exhorts them to "love their wives *as their own bodies*" (v. 28). They need to be thoughtful—to *think* about their wives' needs and actively try to meet them, just as they care for their own needs. As Paul says, "He who loves his wife loves himself. For no one ever hated his own flesh, but nourishes and cherishes it, just as Christ does the church" (vv. 28-29). Men need to recognize that they are one flesh with their wives and to love their wives as they love their own flesh, nourishing and cherishing them as Christ does the church.

Women, on the other hand, have a way of being controlling and manipulative. We may not have the physical strength or the authoritative power of a man, but we do know how to get our own way. We can exert subtle control by being scheming or passive-aggressive. We play games to get men to bend, and we know all the tricks in the book, like crying, nagging, and sulking. Therefore Paul exhorts women to be submissive and respectful toward their husbands *from the heart*, not with ulterior motives, not in a manipulative way, but with the same genuine honor they would give to Christ. When both partners are doing their part, the wife feels cherished, the husband feels respected, and both grow in holiness.

In the healthiest marriages I know, the whole business of authority and submission is practically a non-issue; the husband does not lord it over his wife, and the wife does not manipulate her husband. Rather, they are in an intricate dance. Both partners know each other, know their moves, and stay in step with one another. The husband may often take the lead—not to dominate but to love and guide—and the wife willingly flows with him. Other times it is wise for the husband to acknowledge that the wife should take the lead, and he humbly defers to her. If both are loving one another as they ought, there is no room for either authoritarianism or manipulation. In the best marriages there is such a mutual submission between husband and wife that there is no hierarchy, only harmony. One or the other may be wiser or more skilled in a particular area, but together they are better than either one alone.

Don't forget humor!

shoeboxblog.com

---

[1] From Carl F. George, *Prepare Your Church for the Future* (Tarrytown: Revell, 1991), 129.

LET US RUN WITH PERSEVERANCE

It was a tough day to run a marathon—raw and rainy and windy—but thousands of incredible athletes did it in Boston on April 20, 2015. 30,000 runners—30,000 stories of hardship and endurance and spirit. Here are a few of their stories:

Fourteen years earlier, Laura Joyce of Minnesota had run the Boston Marathon. That weekend she met Nate Davis, whose family has been close to ours since he was five years old. Nate and Laura fell in love, got married, had two babies, trained like crazy, and came back from their home in California to run Boston together. I was thrilled to be able to give both of them their medals.

Laura with a big smile, even though she is frozen to the bone   Nate receiving his medal

Thousands of runners do the Marathon to honor someone special or raise money for a cause. Members of Team MR8, including actor Sean Astin and women's wheelchair winner Tatyana McFadden, ran in memory of eight-year-old Marathon bombing victim Martin Richard, to promote his message of peace and raise money for charitable causes. Tom Feller, son of my high school classmate Deborah Morrison Feller, ran the marathon again this year to raise money for a school for kids with autism. Jessica Brovold ran for Home Away Boston, which provides housing for families with seriously ill children. Her own little daughter Kallie was diagnosed with a brain tumor when she was four years old, and Home Away Boston provided housing for the family when they came from South Dakota to get treatment for Kallie.

All marathon runners have obstacles to tackle, but some are particularly inspirational. A year before the 2015 Marathon, Richard Nasser was in a coma on life support, with doctors unsure whether he would even survive. He not only survived massive injuries, but miraculously started running again competitively within months. At the finish line of the Marathon, he knelt down and proposed to his girlfriend.

I gave a medal to a blind runner and asked if I could take his picture. I later learned he was Randy Pierce, who overcame not only blindness but also a neurological disease that put him in a wheelchair for one year, eight months, and 21 days.

Randy Pierce with teammates

And the last person to finish the Marathon was just as much a winner as the first person to cross the finish line. Maickel Melamed of Venezuela, just one week shy of his fortieth birthday, pressed on through the night and completed the race at 5 a.m. the next day. Melamed suffers from muscular dystrophy, which causes progressive muscle weakness and eventually death. Having lost a nephew to muscular dystrophy at age 16, I am astounded that someone with this debilitating disease could even take one step at age 40, never mind take part in such a grueling test.

And on the Saturday before Marathon Monday, another group of remarkable people did the "Tough Ruck," a marathon course through Minuteman National Historical Park in Concord, Massachusetts. Tough Ruckers, who carry full packs as they race to honor military heroes and raise money for their families, were among the first to help those who were injured in the bombings two years ago. When backpacks were banned in the Marathon after 2013, the Tough Ruck changed venue. This year it was open to civilians for the first time, so my daughter Christine participated. The Tough Ruck is done in partnership with the Boston Athletic Association, so the finishers earn the same well-deserved medal.

Chrissy with Carlos Arredondo, the man in the cowboy hat who helped the injured at the finish line after the 2013 Boston Marathon bombings

Few of us will ever run an actual 26.2-mile marathon. But for every one of us, life is a race with its own obstacles and hardships. We all have to face our own handicaps and climb our own "Heartbreak Hill." Whatever our challenges, "let us run with patience the race that is set before us, looking unto Jesus the author and finisher of our faith" (Heb. 12:1-2).

Those who hope in the LORD will renew their strength.
They will soar on wings like eagles; they will run and not
grow weary, they will walk and not be faint (Isa. 40:31).

IN THE BEGINNING...

Anumber of years ago a friend challenged me to read the book *Darwin's Dangerous Idea* by Daniel Dennett, who is an atheist. I dutifully slogged through the book in order to be able to dialog with my friend. Dennett has no use

NGC 2237 Rosette

for God or the supernatural, and in his book he goes to great lengths to explain how order and complexity, including all the intricacies of human life, can arise out of chaos by purely natural processes, with no supernatural agency.

Dennett may be a brilliant scientist and have a pedigree a mile long, but he has missed the central fact of the universe— that God created the heavens and the earth. The universe has not existed forever—it had a beginning—and it did not come into being by itself—it had a Creator. The Bible makes it clear, and we all know intuitively, that all this beauty and order and intricacy and immensity did not simply happen by chance.

As Christians we all agree about *who* made the heavens and the earth. As we study Scripture, we also learn *why* God brought the world and humanity into existence. But the Bible does not really tell us *how* or *when*. Science has attempted to answer those questions, but no one was there when it happened, no one observed it, no one can reproduce it, no one can test it, and it happened a long time ago, so we can't *prove* what happened. There are several explanations that could fit within the broad framework that God did it, and there are

Bible-believing Christians who hold each of these positions. I present these views not to make a pronouncement about which one is true, but rather to provide a greater understanding of the diverse viewpoints held by fellow believers. My hope is that readers would thoughtfully consider the ideas of other Christians and be charitable toward brothers and sisters with whom they disagree.

The term **Big Bang** was originally used as a sarcastic reference to this theory, which seemed foolish at the time but is now generally accepted among scientists. There is scientific evidence that the universe had its origin in a tremendous explosion nearly 14 billion years ago. All the matter that exists was packed into one point, and when it exploded the matter went hurtling out into space, where it formed stars, galaxies, and planets. The expansion of the universe continues to this day. The Big Bang theory is compatible with the biblical teaching that the created world had a beginning, and many Christians believe that it could be a legitimate scientific explanation of how the universe started.

Perhaps just as astounding as the creation of the entire universe is what happened right here on our little planet, where God chose to concentrate His creative energy, which is actually the focus of most of Genesis 1 and has generated an enormous amount of controversy. Although there is some overlap  among the different theories and there are variants of each, I will try to summarize the views that Christians hold of how our planet and the life on it came to be.

One big divide between Christians on this issue is between **Young Earth Creationists** and **Old Earth Creationists**. Those who believe in a young earth take Genesis 1 literally— that God created the world in six 24-hour days, each marked by evening and morning. They do not accept scientific theories that try to leave God out of the picture and therefore require long geologic eras to allow time for evolution. Young earth creationists calculate the age of the earth by using the biblical genealogies. Even allowing for the gaps in the genealogies, the age of the earth would be on the order of 10,000 years. Just as Adam and Eve were created as adults, so the universe was created with an appearance of age. And just as the second Adam—Jesus—was a specific person at a point in history, so was the first Adam.

Those who believe in an old earth accept the scientific dating methods that say the earth is billions of years old, but they have different models for explaining how science and Genesis fit together. According to the **Framework Hypothesis**, Genesis 1 is not meant to be chronological but is a literary and symbolic structure for God's creative work. This theory recognizes the correspondence between the days of creation: on Day 1 God created light, on Day 4, the lights in the heavens—the sun, moon, and stars; on Day 2 He created the sea and sky, on Day 5, the creatures in the sea and sky; on Day 3 He created the dry land, on Day 6, the creatures on the land. This parallelism suggests that Genesis 1 is presenting a general framework for God's creative acts.

According to the **Gap Theory**, the universe was created billions of years ago, but then there was a long gap during which the geological ages occurred, there was a cataclysm that caused the earth to become "formless and empty," and all of the life-forms that

Bubble Nebula

existed at the time became extinct. Then in Genesis 1:3, God began the work of *re*-creating the earth from its formless and empty state. This theory requires a somewhat strained interpretation of Genesis 1:2, but it accounts for the age of the earth, the geological eras, and the fossil record, as well as the existence of a real Adam and Eve.

Day-Age Creationists say that the "days" in Genesis 1 are not ordinary 24-hour days but long periods of time. They correctly point out that the word *day* in the Bible sometimes means literal 24-hour days and other times means periods of indeterminate length. **Progressive Creationism** accepts the long ages of the earth but rejects Darwin's theory of evolution, which says that species have evolved through natural processes and that humans came from lower life forms. They say instead that the species came into being by special creative acts of God. **Theistic Evolutionists**, on the other hand, hold that evolution is true, but God is the one who designed the mechanism and oversees the process. Because evolution is so often connected to atheism and the desire to do away with God, some Christians who believe in theistic evolution prefer to use a different term for it. Francis Collins, a Christian physician-geneticist who led the Human Genome Project, calls it "BioLogos," which means "Life-Word."

The term **Intelligent Design (ID)** refers to the idea that the mysteries of the universe and of life are best explained by an intelligent cause, not an unguided process. ID is not a religious theory but is an attempt to detect whether the apparent design in nature (which most scientists acknowledge) is the product of a purposeful mind or is simply the result of an undirected process. Proponents of ID say the universe is so perfectly fine-tuned that the probability of all the pieces coming together by chance is essentially zero. Although Intelligent Design is not based on the Bible, Christians will recognize the God of the Bible as the wise Creator who designed the universe.

These hypotheses are just the broad categories; there are many variants of each. Maybe some of these questions, like the time frame of creation, just have to remain in the realm of mystery. Theologically we know that God is timeless, so time for God is not like time for us; "one day" from His perspective could be millions of years from ours. Scientifically we know that time does very weird things at ultra-high densities and ultra-high speeds, which would have been the case in the

Big Bang. We may never be able to put it all together, but the important thing for us is to stand in awe of the grandeur of God's work, what one writer called "the majesty and simplicity of the record of creation."

(All photographs courtesy nasa.gov. The photos from NASA speak eloquently of the wisdom and majesty and power of the Creator.)

Summary:
Theories of Creation Held by Bible-Believing Christians

Big Bang Theory: The universe began as the explosion of an extremely hot and dense point that contained all the matter that exists, which then went hurtling out into space and cooled to form stars, galaxies, and planets.

Young Earth Creationism: The universe has the appearance of great age but was created in six 24-hour days less than 10,000 years ago.

Old Earth Creationism: Accepts the scientific consensus that the earth is billions of years old.

> **Framework Hypothesis:** Genesis 1 is not meant to be chronological but is a literary and symbolic structure for God's creative work.

> **Gap Creationism:** The universe was created billions of years ago, but there was a gap after Genesis 1:1, allowing time for the ordering of the universe, the fall of Satan, the geologic ages, etc. Genesis 1:3ff describes the relatively recent re-creation of Earth.

> **Day-Age Creationism:** The "days" in Genesis 1 represent long periods of time.

> > **Progressive Creationism:** Long ages have passed since the creation of the universe, but the species came into being at certain times by special creative acts of God.

Theistic Evolution (similar to **Evolutionary Creationism**): God is responsible for the development of life on earth, but He has done it through evolutionary processes, like natural selection, as described by science.

Intelligent Design: Features of the universe and of human life point to an intelligent cause; random natural processes with no purpose behind them cannot account for mysteries like the properties of DNA and the fine-tuning of the universe that makes life possible.

SARAH OBEYED ABRAHAM, CALLING HIM LORD

The instructions to wives in 1 Peter 3 can be offensive to women of the twenty-first century, particularly verse 6, which says, "Sarah obeyed Abraham, calling him lord." I have often heard this verse explained with reference to Genesis 12 and the similar story in Genesis 20, where Abraham told Sarah to say she was his sister, not his wife. Abraham's plan is generally seen in a negative light. The explanation of Genesis 12:11–13 in the ESV Study Bible notes is typical:

> Fearful that his life will be endangered because of Sarai's beauty, Abram devises a ruse, based on a half-truth (see 20:12). Abram's selfish actions imply that he thinks God is unable to protect him. Yet when the plan backfires, it is the Lord who rescues him (12:17).

Peter commends Sarah for her obedience, so if he has these situations in mind as he writes these words, the implication is that a wife should submit to her husband even when he is doing something that is ethically questionable. I have heard just such teaching from a number of sources, and perhaps you have too.

However, other scholars believe that Abraham was implementing a wise plan to protect Sarah, not a devious scheme to save his own skin. Dr. Gordon Hugenberger, a seminary professor and the senior pastor of Park Street Church in Boston, has studied extensively both the Scriptures and the culture in which these events took place, and he concludes that

Abraham and Sarah were acting righteously. He explains that, according to Ancient Near Eastern marriage law, a man's wealth would not go to his sister upon his death, so there would be no financial incentive for Pharaoh or for Abimelech to knock off Abraham and take Sarah as his wife. Dr. Hugenberger also gives many other reasons from the biblical text and from the cultural context to assert that both Abraham and Sarah were conducting themselves uprightly.

If this understanding is correct, then 1 Peter 3:6 becomes much less problematic. Sarah was not compromising any moral values, like honesty and integrity, to be supportive of Abraham; she was cooperating with him to carry out a wise and sensible plan to protect their lives and their inheritance so that God could fulfill His purposes in them. She was, in fact, being a godly wife—doing good and acting with pure conduct. As Abraham's partner and helper, she was showing her love and respect for him. As he explained to Abimelech,

> And when God had me wander from my father's household, I said to her, *"This is how you can show your love to me*: Everywhere we go, say of me, 'He is my brother'"* (Gen. 20:13).

However, there is another consideration. As I examined the 1 Peter passage more closely, I realized that there is nothing in the passage to indicate that Peter was thinking of the sister-wife incidents when he wrote that Sarah obeyed Abraham. So I started wondering, "What *did* Peter have in mind when he wrote these words?" Perhaps he was thinking of her general manner of life; as my husband pointed out, she was a remarkable woman in that she left home and family and everything familiar to follow her husband to an unknown country for an unknown duration (which turned out to be the rest of her life). The Lord spoke to Abram and told *him* to "go from your country and your kindred and your father's house to the land that I will show you," but we have no record that He spoke directly to Sarah with these instructions. So she was following Abraham, wherever he went and whatever he did, as he pursued God on what may at times have seemed to her like a wild goose chase. Her faith and obedience were certainly commendable.

Or maybe he did have a specific incident in mind. I wondered, Does the Bible tell of a time when Sarah called Abraham lord? The cross-references in my Bible to the phrase "calling him lord" took me to Genesis 18. This is the account of the three visitors coming to Abraham to tell him that he would become a father. He immediately went into the tent and told Sarah to fix them some food right away:

> And Abraham went quickly into the tent to Sarah and said, "Quick! Three seahs of fine flour! Knead it, and make cakes" (v. 6).

Sarah was an elderly woman and she may have been resting, since the visitors arrived right "in the heat of the day," but there is no indication that she put up a fuss when her husband asked her to make the cakes. Wives, has your husband ever brought home unexpected visitors who needed to be fed? It might be annoying to drop what we're doing and prepare food for them, but doing it cheerfully is one way to honor our husbands. (Of course, they could also honor us by giving us a heads-up or bringing take-out!)

Then the Lord Himself revealed to Abraham that he would have a son. Abraham believed the promise, but Sarah overheard it and laughed, thinking it was craziness. It is here that she refers to him as her lord:

> So Sarah laughed to herself saying, "After I am worn out, and *my lord* is old, shall I have pleasure?" (v. 12)

Sarah had very logical reasons to doubt such a far-fetched promise:

> Abraham and Sarah were old, advanced in years. (v. 11)

> The way of women had ceased with Sarah. (v. 11)

> "After I am worn out, and my lord is old, shall I have pleasure?" (v. 12)

"Shall I indeed bear a child, now that I am old?" (v. 13)

Abraham and Sarah were advanced in years, old and worn out, and Sarah had long since stopped having her periods. *Of course* they couldn't have a baby! But the LORD Himself said, "Is anything too hard for the LORD? And of course the answer is a resounding *NO!*

So what happened? Abraham believed the promise, but Sarah was dubious. She could not wrap her head around the idea that at this stage of her life she could "have pleasure." She knew she would never experience the joy of having her own baby, and she probably doubted she could even have pleasure with her husband. I wouldn't be surprised if they hadn't had sex in years—her periods had stopped, she was well beyond the age of childbearing, they were both old and worn out, so why bother?

But Abraham laid hold of the promise by faith. I picture him coming to Sarah and saying, "Honey, the LORD Himself promised us a baby. Let's get it on tonight!" She may have been skeptical, but the fact is *she did it*—and the rest is history. She honored her husband and expressed her faith in God, however shaky, by *doing* what it took to conceive the promised child. The idea that Peter may have had Genesis 18 in mind is also supported by the fact that Hebrews commends Sarah's faith to receive power to conceive:

> By faith Sarah herself *received power to conceive*, even when she was past the age, since she considered him faithful who had promised" (Heb. 11:11).

If it is true that Peter has in mind the events of Genesis 18, then Sarah is being commended not for going along with her husband in some shady scheme, as a common interpretation of the Peter passage would have us believe, but for doing her part in God's plan for their lives out of *respect for her husband and faith in God.* This is a model that we can wholeheartedly emulate.

"HE MAKES THE BARREN WOMAN
A JOYFUL MOTHER OF CHILDREN"

Many years ago I read a book about one woman's journey through infertility, loss, and finally, motherhood. It was heart-wrenching to read of her intense yearning for a child, her initial inability to conceive, the daily reminders of her barrenness, and then multiple miscarriages. Already having several children of my own, I knew I couldn't completely comprehend, but it occurred to me at the time that never having children could be just as heart-rending as losing your children. Never having lost a child either, I can only imagine the intense grief and despair it causes, but I don't *think* it would make me wish my children had never been born; in other words, I wouldn't consider it preferable that they had never come into the world at all. Despite the unbearable pain of such a loss, no one could take away from me the joy I had already experienced with them—carrying tiny new life in my womb, the thrill of birth, the delight of watching them grow. And I would still have the hope of being with them for eternity. Those who are childless, on the other hand, never experience those joys and do not have the hope of being together eternally, only the unremitting pain caused by the loss of the little person they have dreamed of.

I know that suffering cannot be quantified or ranked, and I'm not trying to compare degrees of suffering, but rather to encourage empathy and sensitivity toward those who long for children but can't have them. As many as one in six couples struggle with fertility issues, and often their affliction goes unnoticed. For those who are unable to conceive, there is no traumatic "event" that others can recognize, no opportunity to receive an outpouring of sympathy, just the ongoing ache that never goes away, the longing for an event that never happens. Having children myself, I'm afraid I have too often been oblivious to the pain of those who don't, but two recent conversations brought this issue to the forefront—one with my friend Beth who has turned forty and knows that her desire for children of her own will go unfulfilled, and another with my friends David and Neesha, who have experienced ten years of infertility. They represent the millions of people who share this heartache, people you probably pass by every day.

As Christians, what hope can we offer to those who long for a baby but have empty arms year after year? Some come to terms with never having a baby. And there are many wonderful stories of infertility and loss followed by the blessing of a baby. But for many others, the clock keeps ticking until all hope is gone. They have to go on with no prospect of a child in this life. But what about the next?

Consider what the Bible says: We know that one day there will be no more sorrow or mourning or tears (Rev. 21:4), so I think it is safe to say that in that day there will be no unfulfilled longings. Either the longing will be fulfilled, or God will take away the longing, so that no one feels any loss or emptiness or dissatisfaction. In this life, we all yearn for something that is not a present reality: the quadriplegic longs to walk; the mother whose little child has been kidnapped and murdered longs to hold him again; the person who has been sick his whole life longs to be made well; someone who has been neglected and abused longs for acceptance and compassion. Knowing that God's heart is to bless His children, we can confidently assure these people that He will grant them what they have longed for and take away all their grief and heartache and suffering and make them fully satisfied.

And what about the woman who longs more than anything to have a baby but is unable? Like Hannah in 1 Samuel 1, she experiences deep anguish and yearning. Notice the phrases that describe Hannah's pain:

Hannah wept and would not eat (v. 7).

Her heart was sad (v. 8).

She was deeply distressed and prayed to the Lord and wept bitterly (v. 10).

She spoke to the Lord about her affliction (v. 11).

She felt forgotten (v. 11).

She was troubled in spirit (v. 15).

She poured out her soul before the Lord (v. 15).

She spoke out of her great anxiety and vexation (v. 16).

In Hannah's case, God opened her womb and gave her children and took away her sadness in this life, but what of those who never experience this joy? Will we tell the quadriplegic he will walk again and the bereaved mother she will see her child again and the sickly person he will be made whole, but not tell the childless woman that *her* deepest longing will be fulfilled? Will God heal the disease or injury or condition that makes her unable to have children but still not give her any children? We can't make any guarantees, and perhaps God will take away her longing and give her complete contentment in Himself, but maybe there is hope that someday she will experience the joys of motherhood. Although we can't know for sure, I think we do well to err on the side of *extravagant hope* based on God's *extravagant love*. We don't know the specifics of what He has in store, but what we do know is that what He is preparing for us is far beyond what we can begin to imagine.

> But as it is written, Eye hath not seen, nor ear heard, neither have entered into the heart of man, the things which God hath prepared for them that love him (1 Cor. 2:9).

Now to him who is able to do immeasurably more than all we ask or imagine, according to his power that is at work within us, to him be glory in the church and in Christ Jesus throughout all generations, for ever and ever! Amen (Eph 3:20-21).

He settles the childless woman in her home as a happy mother of children. Praise the LORD! (Ps. 113:9).

THREE-MINUTE THEOLOGY

I f you had three minutes to describe the attributes of God, what would you say? How could you capture the essence of who God is in a concise statement?

Peter tells us that "God's divine power has granted to us all things that pertain to life and godliness, through the knowledge of him who called us to his own glory and excellence" (2 Pet. 1:3). If we have everything we need for life and godliness *through the knowledge of him who called us,* what is it that we need to *know* about God in order to live the way He intended?

Once God has spoken; twice have I heard this: that power belongs to God, and that to you, O Lord, belongs steadfast love.
Ps. 62:11-12

I believe there are two essential qualities that we need to understand about God: that He is *good* and that He is *sovereign.* Jeremiah tells us what we need to understand about God's goodness:

> Let him who boasts boast in this, that he understands and knows me, that I am the Lord who practices *steadfast love, justice, and righteousness* in the earth. For in these things I delight, declares the Lord (Jer. 9:24).

Jeremiah declares that God is *loving, just,* and *righteous.* His heart is good and kind, His actions are right, and His character is holy.

But the fact that God is good does not necessarily mean that He has the ability to make good happen. He could be a kindhearted grandfather who is virtuous but weak. But we know that God is also *sovereign.* Peter refers to His sovereignty as "His divine power" (1:3).

By itself, the fact that God is sovereign does not necessarily mean that He will do what is good. He could be an all-powerful but cruel despot. But the truth that God is *both* good and sovereign means that He is *willing and able* to work all things together for good, and knowing that truth gives us assurance that He *will* do it. Herein lies our hope that He will fulfill all "His precious and very great promises" (2 Pet. 1:4).

The Psalmist states something similar in Psalm 62. He introduces his statement with the words "Once God has spoken; twice have I heard this," a Hebrew construction that emphasizes the certainty of what is being declared.

> Once God has spoken; twice have I heard this: that *power* belongs to God, and that to you, O Lord, belongs *steadfast love* (Ps. 62:11-12).

In other words, the Psalmist confirms that God is both powerful and loving. As we grasp the meaning of these two qualities, we can trust in Him with full assurance of faith.

Psalm 145 also confirms God's goodness and sovereignty, and that because of these qualities, He will certainly do what is good. Many phrases speak of His power and greatness:

> greatness that no one can fathom
> mighty acts
> the glorious splendor of your majesty
> the power of your awesome works
> your great deeds
> the glory of your kingdom
> your might

> the glorious splendor of your kingdom
> dominion that endures through all generations

And His goodness is also declared over and over:

> your abundant goodness
> your righteousness
> gracious and compassionate
> slow to anger and rich in love
> good to all
> compassion on all He has made
> loving toward all He has made
> righteous in all His ways

Therefore we can trust that He is willing and able to *do* good:

> wonderful works
> faithful to all His promises
> upholds all those who fall
> lifts up all who are bowed down
> gives food at the proper time
> opens His hand and satisfies our desires
> near to all who call on Him
> fulfills the desires of those who fear Him
> hears our cry and saves us
> watches over all who love Him

So if I had three minutes to describe the key attributes of God, I would focus on His *goodness* and His *sovereignty*. What is your three-minute theology?

DO WE WORSHIP THE SAME GOD?

In a Sunday school class I attended we explored the question "Do Muslims and Christians worship the same God?" Many Bible-believing Christians would be quick to answer "no." But a quick answer to this question reflects a failure to grapple with the many nuances and ramifications of the problem. It is a critical theological question that deserves thoughtful consideration. And it is not simply a theoretical question; it has practical implications for how we live. How does the answer affect the way we view and treat Muslims, the way we interact with them, the way we witness to them?

I will not attempt to answer this question but rather will raise some more that are prompted by this one, in hopes of stimulating thoughtful dialog on this important topic. For example,

> How similar do your views of the character of God have to be in order to say that you worship the *same* God?

> How alike do your views have to be in order to worship *together*?

> How accurate does your understanding of God have to be in order to say that you worship the *true* God?

These questions affect our interaction not just with Muslims and others of different faiths, but also with fellow Christians. For example, I have been told by some Calvinists that I worship a different god. It is true that our concepts of God are quite different; what are the implications for our fellowship and worship?

Perhaps the most striking difference is in our views of the love of God. Some Calvinists, like A. W. Pink, simply assert that God does *not* love everyone: "God loves whom He chooses. He does not love everybody" (*The Sovereignty of God*). Other Calvinists, like John MacArthur, believe that Pink went too far. They attempt to correct the error by affirming the biblical truths that God is love and that He loves because He chooses to love. They believe that God grants common grace to all ("He causes his sun to rise on the evil and the good, and sends rain on the righteous and the unrighteous," Mt. 5:45), and that His offers of mercy to the unsaved are "sincere expressions of the heart of a loving God."

However, most Calvinists think there is a sharp distinction between God's love for the elect and His love for everyone else. As MacArthur notes,

> [I]t is folly to think that God loves all alike, or that He is compelled by some rule of fairness to love everyone equally.... [A]n important distinction must be made: God loves believers with a particular love. God's love for the elect is an infinite, eternal, saving love.... Such love clearly is not directed toward all of mankind indiscriminately, but is bestowed uniquely and individually on those whom God chose in eternity past.[1]

I do not share the Calvinists' view of the love of God. His love toward one group of people is not different from His love toward the rest of humanity. God *is* love. Love is His very nature, and it does not change depending on the object. He does not show "an infinite, eternal, saving love" toward some and a lesser love toward others. As I have stated before,

> God is love, He always operates in love, He loved us while we were sinners, and He will always love us. And by "us" I mean the whole human race. And by "love" I mean the quality that in God is infinitely higher and purer than the best human love but *not* radically different from it nor unrecognizable as love.

And by "always" I mean that He will never stop loving us—not when we sin, not when we rebel against Him, not when we die.

So we have two divergent views of a key attribute of God. Are we talking about different Gods, or about differing perceptions of the one God? Can we worship together when the object of our worship is so very different in a major respect? *All* of us have faulty, inadequate views of the God we worship; how do we determine which views are close enough to the truth to be considered worship of the true God?

For my part, I cannot worship God as He is perceived by Calvinists with respect to His fundamental nature of love. Contemplating a God who withholds His "infinite, eternal, saving love" from the majority of humanity does not produce adoration in me. If God "loves" people enough to grant a certain level of providence to them but not enough to die for them, then such "love" is less than it could be—not worthy of an infinitely holy and infinitely loving Lord.

However, I can worship *with* Calvinists. We have enough in common—particularly regarding the sovereignty of God, the holiness of God, the person of Christ, and the power of the cross—that we can (in my opinion) lift our praises to Him together, while envisioning Him in our own way.

The situation with Muslims and Christians is not parallel, but we need to be asking the same kinds of questions as I have raised here. I will leave it to readers to carry on the conversation by asking and thoughtfully trying to answer these and other questions. I would just ask that your goal not be to prove a point or win a theological argument, but rather to consider how best to advance the Kingdom of God.[2]

[1] MacArthur, John. *The God Who Loves* © 2001

[2] My sister Jan, who is a pastor, made this observation from her experiences with people of other faiths in her community: "Muslims and Christians certainly can and should work together, play together, and serve together. I personally think it compromises the integrity of people of both religions to try to worship together."

BE LIKE YOUR HEAVENLY FATHER...
LOVE YOUR ENEMIES

If we actually listen to the Scripture readings in church, they can be annoyingly convicting. One Sunday the Epistle reading was Romans 12:9−21. These thirteen verses contain some thirty (count 'em!) directives about how we should live. As in all his epistles, Paul is presenting kingdom values—the standards for living in the Kingdom of God—which are usually at odds with worldly values.

Throughout His ministry, Jesus taught the true ways of God, which often meant *un*teaching the false ideas held by the people. We see this correction in the Sermon on the Mount, where Jesus' pattern is "You have heard..., *but I say to you...*" Over and over He states a commonly accepted idea and then proceeds to give the true understanding of that concept. He is not abolishing the Law; rather, He is fulfilling it and teaching what it really means (Mt. 5:17).

One thoroughly mistaken notion that Jesus and Paul tried to correct was about how to treat one's enemies. In Romans 12, Paul counters commonly accepted beliefs by saying

Bless those who persecute you; bless and do not curse (v. 14).

Never pay back evil for evil to anyone (v. 17).

If possible, so far as it depends on you, be at peace with all men (v. 18).

If your enemy is hungry, feed him, and if he is thirsty, give him a drink (v. 20).

Do not be overcome by evil, but overcome evil with good (v. 21).

In the Sermon on the Mount, Jesus states the misconception and then His command:

You have heard that it was said, "You shall love your neighbor and hate your enemy." But I say to you, love your enemies and pray for those who persecute you, so that you may be sons of your Father who is in heaven (Mt. 5:43-45).

The same principle is given in Luke 6:

I say to you who hear, love your enemies, do good to those who hate you, bless those who curse you, pray for those who mistreat you (Lk. 6:27-28).

Jesus even said that the principle of love for God and neighbor underlies and summarizes the entire Law:

"Teacher, which is the great commandment in the Law?" And He said to him, "'You shall love the Lord your God with all your heart, and with all your soul, and with all your mind.' This is the great and foremost commandment. The second is like it, 'You shall love your neighbor as yourself.' On these two commandments depend the whole Law and the Prophets" (Mt. 22:36-40).

When Jesus talked about our neighbors, He didn't just mean the folks who live next door. He meant our fellowmen, the whole human race. The Jews thought they were supposed to love just fellow Jews (and maybe not even all of them!), but Jesus expanded the command to include Samaritans and Romans and Gentiles of all kinds—the whole world.

In correcting the Jews' understanding of how to treat their enemies, Jesus was also correcting their understanding of how God treats *His* enemies. Our love is to be a reflection of the infinitely greater love of God. Our love for our enemies is evidence that we are children of a loving God:

I say to you, love your enemies…, so that you may be sons of your Father who is in heaven…. You are to be perfect, as your heavenly Father is perfect (Mt. 5:44-48).

But love your enemies, and do good, and lend, expecting nothing in return; and your reward will be great, and you will be sons of the Most High; for He Himself is kind to ungrateful and evil men. Be merciful, just as your Father is merciful (Lk. 6:35-36).

Jesus commands us to love our enemies, do good to those who hate us, and bless those who curse us. Our heavenly Father is the model for this kind of love. Any notions of true love that we may have do not originate within ourselves; they come from God Himself. He is loving, He is perfect, He is kind, He is merciful. He is kind even to ungrateful and evil men. We need to listen to Jesus' words with a humble heart so we can learn who God the Father really is and how we can be like Him. As Paul says,

Follow God's example, therefore, as dearly loved children and walk in the way of love, just as Christ loved us and gave himself up for us as a fragrant offering and sacrifice to God (Eph. 5:1-2).

God is able to bring His whole creation to respond to His inexhaustible love and in turn to worship Him in heartfelt adoration, as proclaimed by the hymn "All Praise to Thee":

All praise to thee, for thou, O King divine,
didst yield the glory that of right was thine,
that in our darkened hearts thy grace might shine.

Thou cam'st to us in lowliness of thought;
by thee the outcast and the poor were sought;
and by thy death was God's salvation wrought.

Let this mind be in us which was in thee,
who wast a servant that we might be free,
humbling thyself to death on Calvary.

Wherefore, by God's eternal purpose, thou
art high exalted o'er all creatures now,
and given the Name to which all knees shall bow.

Let every tongue confess with one accord
in heaven and earth that Jesus Christ is Lord;
and God the Father be by all adored.
Alleluia!

—F. Bland Tucker

And let us pray this Prayer for the Persecuted Church:

O God, the Father of all, whose Son commanded us
to love our enemies: Lead them and us from prejudice
to truth: deliver them and us from hatred, cruelty, and
revenge; and in your good time enable us all to stand
reconciled before you.

"THEY FOUGHT THE GOOD FIGHT, THEY FINISHED THE RACE"

One hundred twenty years of history were packed into the 2016 running of the most famous marathon in the world. More than 30,000 athletes wheeled and ran their way into history, with half a million enthusiastic spectators cheering them on at every step along the 26.2-mile route.

It is a fun run for some—like the guys in tutus or the Elvis impersonator. But for many, it is a very sacred event. They run to overcome personal challenges, to honor a loved one, or to raise money for a cause that is dear to their heart. My friend **Kristen Havey** was running with the Race4Chase team, to support the CMAK Sandy Hook Memorial Foundation, in honor of Chase Michael Anthony Kowalski. As Kristen explained, "The CMAK foundation is named after a talented runner and passionate little boy named Chase. Chase was my daughter Livvie's age when his life was tragically taken as an active shooter entered his school on December 14, 2012. As both a teacher and a parent, the events on this day were heartbreaking for me, but the resilience of those affected was inspiring." Kristen raised over $8,500 to help CMAK in its mission of serving children and families.

Kristen Havey, running for CMAK Sandy Hook Memorial Foundation: "To turn tragedy into triumph by healing and strengthening our families and communities."

Paul Reardon, running for Spaulding's Race for Rehab Team: "Run for those who can't."

Another friend, Paul Reardon, ran for Spaulding Rehabilitation Hospital's Race for Rehab team, and also in memory of his mom: "This year not only am I running in honor of my mom but also for those who can't; those who are fighting their battles with debilitating illness and injury. Those who themselves may have a dream of one day running the Boston Marathon or just going for a walk in the park." In two years of running with the Race for Rehab team, Paul raised over $15,000 to help Spaulding "improve the quality of life for persons recovering from or learning to live fully with illness , injury, or disability."

Always on this day we remember the awful events of Marathon Monday 2013. Two survivors of the Marathon bombings, Patrick Downes and Adrianne Haslet-Davis, ran the race on their prosthetic legs—proof that their spirit, and the spirit of Boston, could not be broken. Patrick's wife, Jessica, who lost both legs in the bombing, was there to greet him at the finish line. Adrianne almost had to drop out, as her prosthesis dug into her stump and caused unbearable pain. But through her own grit and the sustaining power of her many supporters—including President Barack Obama, who tweeted at mid-race, "Thank you, Adrianne, for being Boston Strong. Terror and bombs can't beat us. We carry on. We finish the race!"—Adrianne did finish the race.

Another amputee who made it all the way against the odds was **Earl Granville**, a friend of my daughter Christine. Earl lost his left leg and sustained severe injuries to his

Wounded veteran Earl Granville: "Keep fighting the good fight." Photo credits: Bradley Rhoton

right leg in a roadside bombing in Afghanistan in 2008. Two years later, he lost his twin brother and fellow soldier, Staff Sgt. Joe Granville, who took his own life. Since then, Earl has been a spokesman and advocate for veterans as a member of Operation Enduring Warrior. He has rucked many miles raising money for veteran causes and has run countless obstacle races, encouraging others to overcome their challenges. Two weeks before Boston, Earl broke his hand in a crash while guiding a blind amputee doing a half marathon on a handcycle. And two days before Boston, he did a Spartan obstacle race. Nevertheless, even drained and one-handed, as well as one-legged, he completed the Marathon on a handcycle. He fought the good fight and finished the race!

Andi Marie Piscopo also did the Marathon back-to-back with another grueling event. On Saturday, she did the 25-hour, 40-mile GoRuck Heavy. Then on the morning of Marathon Monday, she wrote, "I promised to carry a few names for some people to honor their sacrifice, but each one of these names listed, will be carrying me. They will motivate me when it hurts, when I want to stop. Well, not today... For You I Will Not Quit." And she did not quit!

Another remarkable event took place on the Saturday before the Marathon. Since backpacks are no longer allowed at the Marathon, members of the military, along with first responders and civilian supporters, now do the Tough Ruck, a 26.2-mile hike along the Battle Road Trail in Concord. Each one carries a 30+-pound pack and a ribbon with the name of a fallen service member or first responder. As their website says, "It is an honor for Ruckers to wear the name of a Fallen Hero on their Ruck Sack and carry that name 26.2 miles and

across the finish line." My daughter Christine did the Tough Ruck for her second time, one of many rucks she has done for veterans.

Chrissy and friends at Tough Ruck: "We Ruck for those who cannot."

140

I wish I could stop to talk to every runner; each one has a unique story. When the runners start flooding in we have only a moment to put the medal around their neck and give them a smile and a word of congratulations and maybe a hug, but there is a connection in that moment and a sharing of their elation. Here are some vignettes:

We always get great appreciation from the runners, but this year I had the honor of receiving a very special gift. After I gave a Korean runner his medal, he handed me this exquisite gold-plated bookmark from the Goodwill Art Shop in Korea. The words on the card read

"for your special memory always you believe,

anything you hope, bookmark it in your life!"

"Anything you hope, bookmark it in your life!"

In my 2015 Marathon account I featured Randy Pierce, a blind runner from Team with a Vision. Here is another blind runner, Michael Somsan, with his teammates. Michael was a medical officer in the army with plans to be a doctor when he lost his sight. Instead of becoming a doctor, he went to law school and now has his own practice as an attorney.

Blind runner Michael Somsan has participated in two Ironmans and more marathons than he can count.

When I saw a runner with "27 in a Row" on his t-shirt, I asked if I could take his picture. I later learned he is Dr. Stephen Reed, age 68, of Wiscasset, Maine. In addition to his twenty-seven consecutive Boston Marathon finishes, he also has a nearly forty-year streak of running at least a mile (and usually three) every day! Except for his bib number (15575), I could have confused Stephen Reed with Bud Wisseman (15583) who, at age 76, was also running in his 27th Boston Marathon in a row!

Stephen Reed, 27 in a Row

When I saw this man, I thought at first that he had ditched his shoes after the race. But no—he ran the whole race barefoot... for the fourth time... at age 74!

Barefoot runner Tyson Park, age 74

And of the tens of thousands of loyal volunteers, some stand out above the rest. Larry Gagnon has been doing it for a long time—it is his nineteenth year with the Boston Marathon, his fifteenth as leader of the medals team—but his enthusiasm never wavers. His motto is "Live life with passion!" and he instills that same zeal into the whole team.

Medals team leader Larry Gagnon: "Live life with passion!"

Another Marathon has come and gone, but the runners will carry the satisfaction of their achievement forever, and we will continue to be inspired by their stories. You may never run an actual marathon, but you undoubtedly have daunting challenges in your own life. You can tackle them with the same resolve and commitment and passion as these athletes, so that, like them, you will be able to say,

"I have fought the good fight, I have finished the race, I have kept the faith." (2 Timothy 1:7)

UNBROKEN

F ew books I have ever read depict the depths of human depravity, the strength of the human spirit, and the surpassing grace of God more powerfully than *Unbroken: A World War II Story of Survival, Resilience, and Redemption.* For good reason, the book was on the *New York Times* bestseller list for more than four years; readers are riveted by the gripping tale and, like me, want to urge others to read it.

Author Laura Hillenbrand, who also wrote *Seabiscuit: An American Legend,* spent seven years meticulously researching the life and times of the legendary hero of her book, Louis Zamperini. Louie was a hell-raiser as a child, but as a teenager he channeled his energy into running and became a world-class track star, making it to the 1936 Summer Olympics in Berlin while still in his teens.

Zamperini enlisted in the U.S. Army Air Forces in 1941 and became a bombardier in the Pacific. Hillenbrand graphically describes the harrowing missions flown by the Pacific airmen. The casualty rate was astronomical, even greater in accidents than in combat. In 1943, Louie and ten other men were sent out on a notoriously unreliable B-24 bomber to look for a lost plane and its crew. The B-24 went down in the Pacific, leaving only Louie and two other survivors on rubber rafts with little food or water.

Day after day and night after night, the men endured agonizing thirst and hunger, blistering heat and numbing cold, terrifying attacks from the ever-present sharks, strafing by a Japanese war plane, and the utter loneliness of being an infinitesimal speck in an immense, unforgiving ocean. One of the men died after 33 days at sea. Louie and the other man drifted for 47 days, covering a distance of 2,000 miles and finally landing in the Marshall Islands, where they were captured by the Japanese. What came next made them long to be back on the raft.

The cruelty that Louie and other POWs faced at the hands of their Japanese captors was even worse than the brutality of nature. Unspeakable horrors were inflicted on them, and Louie was singled out for extra torment because of his celebrity status and his courageous defiance. He remained steadfast through two years of barbaric treatment, until Japan surrendered to the Allies and the POWs were released.

Finally Louie was liberated, but he was not really free. The war followed him home. He suffered from what we now recognize as PTSD, experiencing nightmares, flashbacks, alcoholism, and a thirst for revenge. Then he came to Christ through the young evangelist Billy Graham, and he was truly set free. The nightmares ceased, and he was miraculously able to forgive his

Louie Zamperini with Billy Graham

tormentors. As Laura Hillenbrand put it simply, for Louie Zamperini, the war was over. He became an ambassador for Christ—appealing to people to be reconciled to God and modeling God's forgiveness by forgiving his captors, in some cases even in person.

Louis Zamperini passed away in July 2014, at the age of 97. His life came to the big screen a few months later in the movie adaptation of *Unbroken*, directed by Angelina Jolie. The movie was riveting but did not tell about his conversion. Please read the book or you will miss the most exciting part of the story—the liberation and transformation of a man by the cross of Jesus Christ.

NEFARIOUS

When I read the book *Unbroken* (pg. 143), which documented the treatment of Allied POWs in Japanese prison camps during World War II, I thought it revealed the deepest depths of human depravity. But it may be that there are some who sink deeper still.

While visiting my daughter Joanna, we went to her church for a viewing of the documentary *Nefarious: Merchant of Souls*, which exposes the dark world of human trafficking. The odious practice of buying and selling human beings has been going on since ancient times and is burgeoning today, not just in Asia and Africa, but in developed countries, quite possibly in your own community. Inflicting unspeakable torment on prisoners of war is despicable enough, but kidnapping and violating children is incomprehensibly wretched. As described in the synopsis for *Nefarious*,

> Victims are systematically stripped of their identity, battered into gruesome submission, and made to per-form humiliating sexual acts on up to 40 strangers every night. Most are held in dingy apartments and brothels, forced to take heavy doses of illegal drugs, and monitored very closely. Victims are often thrown into such ghastly oppression at 13 years old. Some are abducted outright, while others are lured out of pov-erty, romantically seduced, or sold by their families.

As Joey thought of her own four little girls, she couldn't bear the idea that other children were being taken from their families and exploited as sex slaves. She resolved to do something about it, and when the opportunity arose to go on a short-term mission trip to Thailand with others from her church and from around the country, she volunteered.

For a year the members of her team prayed and planned and prepared, and then they traveled halfway around the globe to do their part in fighting this monumental injustice. Though the members of a short-term mission team can't make a dent in the estimated 20 million victims of human trafficking, they *can* make a difference in the lives of individual women and children by showing them the love of Jesus and letting them know that they are precious to Him. As the organization they worked with describes its mission,

> We strive to reach every person with the love of God and rescue every child from human trafficking,... to transform each child from her past and give her an opportunity for a better future.

Joey tells about Han (name has been changed), whose story represents countless girls who are longing for a way out of the nightmare of being trapped in sexual slavery:

> Han is a teenage girl who was rescued from a trafficking situation in which she had suffered years of physical, sexual, and emotional abuse. After a few weeks at the home for rescued children, Han asked one of the staff members, "What took you so long?" The staff member thought that Han was asking why she had not been rescued sooner. But Han followed up her initial question with, "Why did I have to wait so long to hear about Jesus?" Despite the atrocities she had experienced, Han's relief was not just for her physical security, but for the new hope that she had found as a dearly loved child of God. A year after I first heard her story, I still can't recount it without tears in my eyes.

We may have thought that slavery ended with the Civil War, but millions of human beings are still trapped. It may seem that God has turned a deaf ear to their cries, but He never forgets a single soul. His heart is especially toward the weak and oppressed.

> Why, O LORD, do you stand far away?
>> Why do you hide yourself in times of trouble?
> Arise, O LORD; O God, lift up your hand;
>> forget not the afflicted.
> O LORD, you hear the desire of the afflicted;
>> you will strengthen their heart; you will incline
>> your ear
> to do justice to the fatherless and the oppressed,
>> so that man who is of the earth may strike terror
>> no more. (Ps. 10:1, 12, 17-18)

Through the efforts of the dozens of organizations working against human trafficking, many are being set free and restored to wholeness. But at present we see only a small foretaste of the full liberation that Jesus will bring about when He returns:

> The Spirit of the Lord is on me,
>> because he has anointed me
>> to proclaim good news to the poor.
> He has sent me to proclaim freedom for the prisoners
>> and recovery of sight for the blind,
> to set the oppressed free,
>> to proclaim the year of the Lord's favor.
>> (Lk. 4:18-19)

"THAT THEY MAY BE ONE"

As we were talking about the concept of Christian unity, my husband reminded me of the words of Merrill C. Tenney, professor of New Testament and Greek and dean of the graduate school of Wheaton College. Dr. Tenney, who received his Ph.D. from Harvard University, also served on the translation team for the New American Standard Bible.

In his commentary *John: The Gospel of Belief*,[1] Tenney discusses Jesus' high priestly prayer in John 17. In His prayer Jesus asks the Father that His disciples might fully experience eternal life, including knowing Him, being protected and kept safe by the power of His name, having the full measure of His joy, and being sanctified by the truth. And as Tenney says, "Unity is another factor in eternal life. The final prayer of Jesus for the believers as a whole was that they should be one (22)." Jesus reiterates this idea over and over in His prayer:

"Father, protect them by the power of your name— **so that they may be one** as we are one" (v. 11).

"I pray also for those who will believe in me through their message, **that all of them may be one**, Father, just as you are in me and I am in you" (v. 21).

"I have given them the glory that you gave me, **that they may be one** as we are one" (v. 22).

"**May they be brought to complete unity** to let the world know that you sent me and have loved them even as you have loved me" (v. 23).

148

So what does it mean "that they may be one"? Let's look first at what it does *not* mean. Tenney says, "A clear distinction should be drawn between four closely allied concepts: unanimity, uniformity, union, and unity." He describes **unanimity** as "absolute concord of opinion within a given group of people." Unanimity is not necessary for unity and in fact is an impossibility; no group of people, Christians or not, will ever be in absolute agreement about even one issue.

Tenney defines **uniformity** as "complete similarity of organization or of ritual." Uniformity is not only unnecessary; it would be unbearably monotonous and suffocating. Imagine an orchestra composed of identical instruments playing the same notes, or churches full of cookie-cutter Christians, all marching in lockstep. Jesus never intended that we all be alike; that's why He created us with different gifts and why His Church has many different expressions.

Tenney says that "**union** implies political affiliation without necessarily including individual agreement." Creating religious organizations will never bring about the unity that Jesus envisioned for His church. His body is not a visible association or agency but rather a living entity.

True **unity**, according to Tenney, "requires oneness of inner heart and essential purpose, through the possession of a common interest or a common life." He goes on to describe what unity looks like:

> Within the church of historic Christianity there have been wide divergences of opinion and ritual. Unity, however, prevails wherever there is a deep and genuine experience of Christ; for the fellowship of the new birth transcends all historical and denominational boundaries. Paul of Tarsus, Luther of Germany, Wesley of England, and Moody of America would find deep unity with each other, though they were widely separated by time, by space, by nationality, by educational background, and by ecclesiastical connections. Such unity was what Jesus petitioned in His prayer,

for He defined it as the unity which obtained between Himself and the Father, "as thou, Father, art in me, and I in thee, that they also may be in us" (21).

What is the purpose of this unity of Christians with God and with one another? It is to be a reflection of God's beauty and a testimony to the world. Jesus asked the Father that His people might be one **"as we are one"** (vv. 11, 22), **"just as you are in me and I am in you"** (v. 21). He prayed, "May they also be in us **so that the world may believe that you have sent me"** (v. 21) and "May they be brought to complete unity **to let the world know that you sent me and have loved them even as you have loved me"** (v. 23).

Unity and love go hand in hand to reveal Christ to the world. As Jesus said to His disciples earlier that same night, "A new command I give you: Love one another. As I have loved you, so you must love one another. **By this all men will know that you are my disciples, if you love one another"** (Jn. 13:34-35). The old sixties song "They'll Know We Are Christians" by Peter Scholtes got it right:

We are one in the Spirit, we are one in the Lord
And we pray that all unity may one day be restored
And they'll know we are Christians by our love.

Tenney concludes his discussion by urging us to pursue true unity in order to faithfully represent God to the world:

Jesus did not pray for absolute unanimity of mind, nor for uniformity of practice, nor for union of visible organization, but for the underlying unity of spiritual nature and of devotion which would enable His people to bear a convincing testimony before the world.

So how convincing is our testimony?

---

[1] Tenney, Merrill C., *John: The Gospel of Belief*, Wm. B. Eerdmans Publishing Company, 1948.

HOMECOMINGS

As the last of our children left to go back to college after Christmas 2011, I found myself thinking about homecomings. The holidays are a time for homecomings—joyous reunions of family and friends from far and near. Here are some vignettes about homecomings. How does your heart respond to them?

As Christmas approached, I was looking forward to having my husband home from the hospital after major surgery and to the arrival of the kids and grand-kids. Only our next-to-youngest son would be missing; he was teaching English in Spain and would not be able to come home because of the distance, time, and expense. But just as we were sitting down for dinner on Christmas Eve, in came Andy from Spain! The kids had orchestrated the surprise, chipped in for his ticket, and arranged for a friend to pick him up at the airport so we wouldn't get suspicious. Then on Christmas Day, we had our whole family together, gathered in Massachusetts from north, south, west, *and* east—New Hampshire, New York, Florida, Indiana, California, and Spain.

Would it really have mattered if only one person out of 16 had been missing? Yes! Of course I was thrilled that so many could come, but there would have been an empty spot if Andy had not been here. The joy would have been tempered by the sadness of knowing that someone was left out. My friend was lamenting that not all her children could be home for Christmas; she wants her daughter to marry a Jewish boy so she doesn't have to share her with the in-laws at Christmastime!

A helicopter rescue pilot from the Australian floods of 2011 also understands all too well that every last person is important. His selfless heroism helped to rescue 28 people, but he is still wracked with grief that some were lost:

> Chopper pilot Mark Kempton turned to look at a pregnant woman he'd just rescued, expecting to see nothing in her face but relief and gratitude. What met his gaze was unspeakable horror. Seconds before she was dragged to safety, she'd lost her grip on her baby. It was snatched away by the unrelenting brown torrent that hit Grantham. For her, the angel of mercy had appeared over the horizon just too late.[1]

It hardly mattered to the mother that she herself had been saved; the joy she would have felt was completely overshadowed because her baby was lost. The pilot felt the agony of not being able to save everyone. He said,

> It's just heartbreaking. It doesn't matter how many people you save, what you do, you always want to just get someone else, one more, you want to get everyone.

The film *Hacksaw Ridge* tells the story of Desmond Doss, a conscientious objector who became a combat medic in World War II. He too understood the value of each person. He kept running back again and again into the brutal battle on Okinawa trying to save his injured squad mates. Each time he ran back into the carnage, he prayed, "One more. Just one more. Lord, please let me get one more." He single-handedly managed to rescue dozens of men presumed to be dead.

In October of 2010, the world held its breath as, one by one, 33 Chilean miners were painstakingly raised from the mine where they had been entombed for 69 days. There was great jubilation as each one was restored to his family. When the last one was raised, the celebration could really begin.

Another marvelous miracle took place in the skies over northwestern Wisconsin on November 2, 2013. As the sun was setting, two planes carrying a total of nine skydivers took off for the last dive of the day. The plan was for the skydivers to jump together and create a formation, but as the planes approached one another, they suddenly collided with a tremendous crash. One plane lost a wing in the fiery explosion and went into an uncontrolled nosedive. The jumpers all managed to jump free of the planes but were still in danger from the flaming debris falling all around them. The pilot of the wingless plane had only two jumps under his belt, but he plunged from the plummeting plane and landed safely. Eventually each of the skydivers came down safely, and then the other pilot skillfully landed his badly damaged plane. The Miracle of the Sunset Dive was that all eleven people survived a catastrophic accident that easily could have killed them all.

What makes the Chilean mine rescue and the Sunset Dive so wonderful and joyous and miraculous is that everybody made it—a teeny foretaste of the day when all God's children will finally be gathered in perfect unity in His eternal home. Picture Jesus descending to the depths of the earth, leading captives in His train, and ascending "higher than all the heavens, in order to fill the whole universe" (Eph. 4:8-10).

God wants *all* of His children to come home, and He sent His Son to die for us to make it possible. He is like Captain Sully, the US Airways pilot who safely landed his plane on the Hudson River after both engines were disabled. All 155 people on board made it out alive. If even one person on Flight 1549 had perished, it would have been a tragedy, but instead that event will always be known as "The Miracle on the Hudson."

Does it break your heart to think of the mother whose baby was swept away in the flood? Or of the Titanic survivors who watched hundreds of others slip away in the icy water? Does it thrill your heart to think of the rescue of the Chilean miners or the passengers of Flight 1549? How much greater the stupendous homecoming that God has in store for us! He reveals in His Word that He is planning a spectacular future, beyond anything we could even imagine. Let your heart leap for joy as you anticipate His gathering of all His people in peace and jubilation.

---

[1] Carswell, Andrew. *Herald Sun*, January 13, 2011.

JOY IS A CHOICE, PART 3

Parts 1 and 2 of this series (pages 59 and 64) presented biblical principles for experiencing joy. Observing and talking with people who live joyful lives has helped me see several more principles.

Love

The most joyful people I know are those who are the most loving. Instead of putting themselves first, they understand the old adage that the key to joy is putting God first and considering others before themselves:

JOY = **J**esus
Others
Yourself

Do nothing out of selfish ambition or vain conceit. Rather, in humility value others above yourselves. Each of you should look not only to your own interests, but also to the interests of others (Phil. 2:3-4).

Studies show that people who cultivate loving relationships and look for opportunities to show kindness are the most content and the most likely to avoid depression. It's for our own wellbeing as well as that of others that we are to love our brothers, love our neighbors, and even love our enemies.

Love your enemies, do good to those who hate you, bless those who curse you, pray for those who abuse you.... Love your enemies, and do good, and lend, expecting nothing in return, and your reward will be great (Lk. 6:27-28; 35).

In all relationships, whether with family or friends or even with colleagues halfway around the world whom you know only through email, treat others with respect and kindness. You'll be pleasantly surprised at how much fun it is to look for ways to show love.

Let all that you do be done in love (1 Cor. 16:14).

Move

While I was talking with my friend Nancy at a party for her fifty-sixth birthday, she was telling me about an idea that has become a theme in her life: "movement." Her goal is to keep moving, both physically and mentally. She has found that making some kind of forward motion every day—doing something a little different or a little better—leads to contentment.

It can start very simply, with small changes, like just taking time to breathe and to notice and enjoy the little pleasures around you. Nancy started walking in the woods near her home, and her short strolls have become long treks. Recently she took me on a walk in her woods and told me more about what she has been learning. She explained that movement clears your mind from the rat race of the world and opens you to take in beauty, which in turn enables you to give out more to other people. Nancy makes it a point to find the worth in every person she meets and to do something each day to enrich someone else's life. Her amazing gardens, which she and her husband created from scratch, provide a place where she can exercise her creative energy and also bring beauty and joy into her corner of the world.

Talking with Nancy inspired me to do something about my far-too-sedentary lifestyle. Since I make my living on a computer, I was spending way too much time on my butt. I knew in my head that for my own physical and emotional health I should be moving more, and I finally decided to do something about it. I bought a board and clamped it to the handles of our old treadmill that had been collecting dust. I put my keyboard and monitor on the board, and voilà—a treadmill desk. Now I walk as I work. The pace is very slow—

barely more than one mile an hour—but it keeps me in motion, and it gives me a sense of wellbeing, both physically and psychologically. I'm trying to be more alert to ways that I can make some forward movement in my life each day.

One of my heroes for staying active is Ruth Colvin. In 1962, Ruth founded Literacy Volunteers of America, now ProLiteracy Worldwide, and she has been a tireless advocate for literacy ever since. She has traveled all over the world to help people learn how to read and write and to teach people how to teach others. In 2006 she received the Presidential Medal of Freedom from President George W. Bush, and the next day she turned 90! She still lifts weights and plays golf regularly and is active in her church and community. I'm sure that her cheerful, upbeat attitude is strongly connected to the fact that she remains active physically and stays engaged in worthwhile endeavors.

Learn

It's important to keep not only your body in gear, but also your brain in gear. Mrs. Colvin is a lifelong learner who keeps her mind active by reading, writing, doing Sudoku puzzles, and participating in book clubs. She is the author of several books, including *Off the Beaten Path: Stories of People Around the World*, which tells some of her adventures meeting people of very different backgrounds and learning about their cultures and traditions.

My nieces Erica and Annie are two of the most talented musicians I know. From early childhood they have dedicated themselves to learning their instruments—Erica the violin and Annie the cello—and today they are incredibly accomplished young women with a bright future in music. Their passion and energy and vibrancy shine through when they play, and it's clear that

Erica

they are having fun! Having the ability to share beautiful music with others brings joy to themselves as well as their hearers.

A study by the Centers for Disease Control and Prevention highlights the connection between keeping your body moving, keeping your mind active, and maintaining a positive outlook. The study suggests that kids who are physically active get better grades and also have a better attitude:

Annie

> Research shows that students who earn mostly **A**s are almost twice as likely to get regular physical activity [as] students who receive mostly **D**s and **F**s. Physical activity can help students focus, improve behavior, and boost positive attitudes.

What's good for kids is good for adults too: keep exercising your body and your brain, and you will view life with more optimism and cheerfulness.

Laugh

After my husband was diagnosed with stage 3 cancer, we decided that we would try to maintain a positive attitude and keep a sense of humor— for our own well-being and for our witness to others. I started a carepages site where I updated family and friends on Tony's condition and posted prayer requests. I included with each

"Yes! That was very loud Mr. Trainer, but I said I wanted to hear your *HEART!*"
© Tucker

post a "Smile for the Day"—something lighthearted, like a joke, anecdote, cartoon, or youtube video that would make people smile. To remind us not to complain, my sister Jan sent us a "No Whining" sign, which we posted in our kitchen. Making a concerted effort to keep a positive focus and a sense of humor helped us get through that tough time.

Jeanne Segal, Ph.D., calls laughter "a powerful antidote to stress, pain, and conflict." She says that "nothing works faster or more dependably to bring your mind and body back into balance than a good laugh. Humor lightens your burdens, inspires hope, connects you to others, and keeps you grounded, focused, and alert." She explains that laughter is good for your health in a variety of ways:

Laughter relaxes the whole body and relieves physical tension and stress.

Laughter boosts the immune system and decreases stress hormones, improving your resistance to disease.

Laughter triggers the release of endorphins, the body's natural feel-good chemicals.

Laughter protects the heart by improving the function of blood vessels and increasing blood flow.

Dare

To keep life interesting and amusing, it's not a bad idea to do something completely nutty and out of your comfort zone once in a while. My daughter got me into obstacle racing, in which participants run a course with a variety of physical challenges and obstacles. So what on earth is a sexagenarian grandma doing climbing over walls, walking across planks, sloshing down a giant slip-'n'-slide, hanging on monkey bars, crawling through mud under barbed wire, and jumping over flames? Doing something goofy to make memories with her daughter and have fun!

A few years ago I went to visit my son Alex in college, and he took me skydiving, which I wrote about in "Fear, Faith, and Freefall" (page 8). I described the experience as "terrifying and exhilarating at the same time." You know there's a certain danger, but you feel fully alive.

When you dare to do something that pushes you past your comfort zone into unknown territory, you discover that you can move beyond what you thought were your limits. You realize that you have strength and inner resources that you didn't know were there, and it gives you more confidence to try the next thing. For you the challenge might be to push yourself physically or conquer a fear or learn a new skill, or maybe to get up the courage to cultivate an unlikely friendship or explore a new idea or pursue a career change. Don't let fear immobilize you!

The joy of the LORD is your strength (Neh. 8:10)

Share

Always focusing inward on yourself and your problems is a sure way to breed self-pity and gloominess. Conversely, reaching out to help others brings satisfaction and joy. My mom, Phyllis Perkins, is a lifelong caregiver and volunteer. As a registered nurse and mother to
five kids, she was always taking care of somebody. For decades she volunteered with many organizations, including her church, Literacy Volunteers, Hospice, Meals on Wheels, Francis House (a home for people with terminal illnesses), and Winds of Agape Home Care Agency, where she helped train certified home health aides.

In 2009, at age 85, she was honored with the Central New York Post-Standard Achievement Award for her outstanding contributions to the community. A year later, she received an honorary doctorate from her college for her service to the Central New York community. Sharing her gifts with others has brought fulfillment and joy, and she can look back with contentment on a life well lived.

Paul commended the believers in Macedonia for giving according to their means and even beyond their means. They found great joy in sharing abundantly, even out of their own poverty:

> We want you to know, brothers, about the grace of God that has been given among the churches of Macedonia, for in a severe test of affliction, **their abundance of joy and their extreme poverty have overflowed in a wealth of generosity on their part**. For they gave according to their means, as I can testify, and beyond their means, of their own accord, begging us earnestly for the favor of taking part in the relief of the saints (2 Cor. 8:1-4).

If your goal in life is your own personal pleasure, it will probably elude you or never be quite satisfying. But if your goal is to love and serve others, you will discover that joy comes as a bonus. Even if you don't have worldly wealth, you can be wealthy in generosity. Share what you do have—if not material resources, then time, talent, or a listening ear—and you will find abundance of joy.

So if you want to experience joy in your life,
practice the biblical principles and remember these keys:

Love—Move—Learn—Laugh—Dare—Share

JOY IS A CHOICE, PART 4

One of the people featured in Part 3 of "Joy Is a Choice" was Ruth Colvin, founder of Literacy Volunteers of America, now called ProLiteracy Worldwide. Ruth has been a model for me not only of joy, but of diligence, perseverance, and selfless service. Here is an update on her life, revealing how she daily continues to exemplify these qualities.

In 2014, Ruth lost her husband, Bob—her best friend, soulmate, and lifelong ministry partner. Experiencing such a loss after being together for so long—they would have celebrated their seventy-fifth wedding anniversary in 2015— would send many into a spiral of depression and loss of hope. But Ruth has chosen to maintain a positive spirit and not to give up on life—even at age 99!

Her 2015 Christmas letter was full of joy and family and thankfulness and purpose:

To family and friends,

A full and busy year, missing Bob (this would have been our 75th anniversary), but working hard to adapt to this new life without him, and counting my blessings.

I'm 99 and thankful that I have good health and am still able to travel. Remember, age is just a number. It's what you do with your number that counts.

Kathie and Vinnie had invited me to Jamaica in January—what a delightful time there. And to California with Lindy and Doug and our California family in February, with Terry and Tammy joining us at Sea Ranch. Family get-togethers are SO important (two new great-grandsons this year). In October, to Lake Placid with Terry, then to the Cape, followed by my going to Charleston, SC for the ProLiteracy national conference. And to DC to celebrate Christmas.

Syracuse is always delightful in the summer, and I made the most of it, playing golf at least three times a week (shorter ball and higher handicap), and going to the gym several times a week. I'm blessed with good friends at church, in my three book clubs, and those on both the LiteracyCNY and ProLiteracy boards.

Reading and writing are still a big part of my life, and I'm teaching again, one-on-one, a young Chinese mother who is a joy to work with. I'm thankful for the computer, emails, iPad and iPhone, so that I can keep in communication with family and friends wherever they are.

God is indeed great and good, and I'm thankful for all the blessings given to me—good health, my loving family, and so many supportive friends.

Blessings to all, with wishes for good health, joy, and peace.

My best to all—Ruth Colvin

Ruth was asked to do a week-long series for the feature "Daily Inspiration" in the city newspaper of Syracuse, New York. She told me, "I hesitated to do it, but decided I've lived a long life and have had thoughts that might help others—so I did it. I was amazed at the response—everyone needs a helping hand."

On November 18, 2016, Ruth was honored with a huge 100th birthday banquet. Hundreds of people came to show their love and respect for a woman who has lived her life well.

There were personal video messages for Ruth from her friend and fellow literacy advocate Barbara Bush and from former President George W. Bush. Tributes were given by a number of dignitaries. A cantata was written especially for her. Over $100,000 was raised for an endowment fund to carry on Ruth's literacy work.

Ruth perseveres by continuing to love, move, learn, laugh, dare, and share. She exemplifies the fact that as long as we have breath, God has a purpose for our lives. Like Ruth, let us "rejoice in the Lord always" (Phil. 4:4) and "let us run with endurance the race that is set before us, looking to Jesus, the founder and perfecter of our faith" (Heb. 12:1-2).

DOES GOD HAVE A SPLIT PERSONALITY?

Critics of the Bible often say that it presents conflicting views of God. They point to descriptions in the Old Testament that paint Him as a God of wrath, and they think He morphs into a nicer God in the New Testament. Even within the New Testament, there are seemingly contradictory images of God. For example, Revelation 14 focuses on God's judgment:

> If anyone worships the beast and its image and receives its mark on their forehead or on their hand, they, too, will drink the wine of God's fury, which has been poured full strength into the cup of his wrath. They will be tormented with burning sulfur in the presence of the holy angels and of the Lamb. And the smoke of their torment will rise for ever and ever. (14:9-10).

Do the descriptions of God's wrath represent one personality, while the descriptions of His love show another? Sometimes it does seem that God has two opposite natures: On the one hand, He is compassionate and forgiving, even sacrificing His own Son for us. He lavishes love on His children and tenderly cares for them. On the other hand, He can appear to be wrathful not only toward His enemies, but even toward His own children. In fact, it's not hard to see why some have maintained that the God of the Old Testament is different in character from the God of the New Testament.

So does God have a split personality? Certainly human beings can manifest different personalities in their actions: Sometimes we react in anger, with no love whatsoever. And sometimes we display a weak love, with no regard for righteousness. But God does not switch from one personality to another. *Everything God does springs from the totality of who He is.* All of His actions reflect His character as a whole.

God never does anything that would violate any part of His character. God is righteous; He can do nothing unrighteous. God is holy; He can do nothing unholy. God is just; He can do nothing unjust. God is merciful; He can do nothing unmerciful. God is love; He can do nothing unloving. All of God's actions are consistent with all of His attributes.

The supreme example of God acting from the fullness of His nature is the cross. There He displayed His wrath against sin, along with His love toward those Jesus died for. *The reason He hates sin is because it hurts the people He loves.* The cross is the perfect expression of who God is.

It's easy to see both God's wrath and His love in the cross. But the cross is not unique in that respect. Though it's often difficult to discern, *everything* God does expresses *all* that He is. So whenever you think you see an angry God at work, be assured that He is in reality exercising His holy love. Even His most severe judgment has a good and loving purpose. As William Cowper wrote in his hymn "God Moves in a Mysterious Way":

Judge not the Lord by feeble sense
But trust Him for His grace.
Behind a frowning providence,
He hides a smiling face.

WHOSE SIDE ARE YOU ON ANYWAY?

With six strong-willed, opinionated children in our family, there was never a lack of conflict in our household when the kids were growing up. I once calculated that with six individuals, there are 57 different combinations of two or more, each with its own unique dynamics. Throw in two stubborn parents, all in a small house with one little bathroom, and you have plenty of potential for clashing of the wills.

Sometimes we would let the kids battle it out on their own, and sometimes we acted as referees. Since I hate conflict, my tendency was to intervene and attempt to reason with the combatants. I would try to help them see each other's viewpoint and come to a mutual understanding. I wanted them to learn to listen, compromise, and get along.

But it often didn't work that way. If I tried to be a mediator between two warring parties, many times I would end up with *both* of them mad at *me*. Each one wanted me to be 100% on their side, to see the justice of their cause and the unreasonableness of the other. Each one wanted me to support him or her completely and to punish the other. Their inability or unwillingness to see through the other person's eyes and to come to a mutual understanding was a reflection of the fact that they were *children*—immature, self-centered children.

Sadly, the same phenomenon happens with adults. We can be contentious and self-absorbed, unwilling to listen thoughtfully, engage in productive dialog, or make any concessions. We want others to agree with us completely, or else they can't be trusted. Liberals are often suspicious of anyone who doesn't buy the entire liberal agenda. Conservatives don't consider you a "true" conservative if you question any part of their ideology. On any controversial issue, we often act like foolish, unreasonable, self-absorbed children. We ought instead to listen carefully as others express their viewpoints, try to grasp all the nuances of a subject, and be ready to suppress our ego without compromising our principles.

When my husband and I were in marriage counseling, there was one piece of advice that was particularly useful. Often both parties approach conflict with the goal of winning the battle—getting their own way or proving that they are right. A much more constructive strategy is to bring your ideas to the table and lay them down. Present the situation as you see it currently, but remain open to additional information and different viewpoints. Instead of acting as adversaries, work as a team to try to put together all the facts and come up with a resolution that is better than what either party started with.

For Christians, the goal is not my will nor the other person's will, but God's will. I may be convinced that *I* know God's will in a matter, but chances are that the other side in a dispute has something to offer. Godly conflict resolution cannot happen without *humility*. Paul admonished us to "do nothing from selfish ambition or conceit, but in humility count others more significant than yourselves" (Phil. 2:3), following the example of Jesus, who "humbled Himself by becoming obedient to the point of death" (Phil. 2:8).

James also has advice about how to get along with others. For one thing, he says we should be "quick to hear, slow to speak, slow to anger" (Js. 1:19). Being "wise and understanding" is shown in "the meekness of wisdom" (Js. 3:13). There is no place for "bitter jealousy" or "selfish ambition" or "boasting" or being "false to the truth" (Js. 3:14). James describes the kind of mature wisdom that is essential for godly relationships and interaction:

CERTAINTY AND UNCERTAINTY

*Now faith is being sure of what we hope for
and certain of what we do not see.*
Hebrews 11:1

Certainty is good. The saints of Hebrews 11 were commended for their faith; they were *sure* of what they hoped for and *certain* of what they did not see. They were still living by faith even when they died without seeing the fulfillment of the promises they were clinging to:

On Being Certain:
Believing You Are Right
Even When You're Not
Robert A. Burton, M.D.
St. Martin's Press, 2008

> All these people were still living by faith when they died. They did not receive the things promised; they only saw them and welcomed them from a distance.... They were longing for a better country—a heavenly one. Therefore God is not ashamed to be called their God, for he has prepared a city for them.

God is pleased when His people exhibit this kind of bold faith—when they steadfastly keep on believing that He will fulfill His promises. Those who have conviction and certainty are held up as models for us; we honor God—and He honors us—when we exercise such faith and assurance.

Luke wrote his gospel and Acts so that Theophilus would know the *certainty* of the things he had been taught:

Therefore, since I myself have *carefully investigated every-thing* from the beginning, it seemed good also to me to *write an orderly account* for you, most excellent Theophilus, so that you may *know the certainty* of the things you have been taught (Luke 1:3-4).

Luke took great pains to search out the facts and get eyewitness reports and write a systematic account so that all of his readers down through the ages could have confidence that what we have been taught about the life of Jesus and the early Church is really true. God wants us to have strong convictions based on fact. The assurance that the facts are true strengthens our faith and gives us boldness to act in obedience to the One who is always true and trustworthy.

And yet, certainty is dangerous. If we are certain we are right, we are less likely to be open to correction and we are at risk for pride. We may cling so tenaciously to our beliefs that we are unwilling to consider other points of view and unable to perceive the nuances of different understandings. We may be uncompromising at times when we should be yielding. Blind faith can lead not only to mistaken ideas but also to actions that are totally out of keeping with the character of the One we profess to follow.

I recall one commenter who insisted that her view in the matter at hand was the only possible understanding that is faithful to Scripture. I asked her, "would you say there is not the slightest possibility that you could be mistaken in your understanding of what Scripture teaches" about this subject? Her response: "None at all." I further questioned her insistence that anyone who takes a view different from hers must be wrong, even if they are questioning not the truth of Scripture but only man's highly fallible translation and interpretation, and she maintained that she could not be wrong in this matter. This kind of attitude with respect to an issue about which genuine Christians disagree is extremely unhealthy.

So how do we make sure we are driven by the right kind of certainty? I have asked myself that question and tried to determine which beliefs I should hold with deep conviction and which ones I should hold more lightly. As my husband and I were discussing this concept, we came up with a thought experiment to test the certainty of our beliefs: Imagine a guillotine with a heavy, razor-sharp blade poised to drop. The guillotine is to be a test not of the truth of your beliefs, but of the strength of the conviction with which you hold them. Would you be willing to put your neck on the chopping block knowing that the blade will drop if your belief is wrong?

For example, I believe with absolute certainty that Jesus rose from the dead—literally, bodily, physically, historically. I would be willing to stick my neck out for that belief, being confident that the blade would not drop. I also believe that God created the heavens and the earth, and I would have no fear about sticking my neck out on that one.

However, I'm not so sure about how or how long ago God created the universe. I would not be willing to put my life on the line for my belief in that area. At the other end of history, I don't know if my understanding of the Second Coming, the Millennium, etc. is correct, and I wouldn't bet my life on it.

We all hold countless beliefs with more or less certainty. We would not even be able to function in life if we did not hold some beliefs with a high degree of certainty. For example, I am virtually 100% sure that the floors in my house will not collapse when I walk on them; without that confidence I would be afraid even to walk in my house. Similarly, I'm quite sure that if I stepped off a bridge the law of gravity would not be suspended for me; that certain knowledge keeps me from doing something stupid.

When it comes to our religious beliefs, we need to be careful about the level of certainty of our convictions. Yes, we need to hold the bedrock doctrines of Christianity—those that constitute the definition of "Christian"—with unwavering faith. But we have to be careful about which doctrines we put in the category of non-negotiables. There are many areas where Christians disagree, and we should be cautious about insisting that our understanding is the only right way.

What beliefs do you hold with complete certainty? What ones do you hold more loosely? Think of each belief you are certain about; is it a hill you want to die on? Think of the beliefs you hold more loosely; do your convictions in those areas need to be strengthened? How do your beliefs and your presentation of them affect your relationships with other Christians? With unbelievers? Do your attitudes honor God? Promote Christian unity? Is your sharing of the gospel clear on the essentials? Is it muddied with non-essentials? Do you need to adjust your level of certainty on any issues?

There's an old joke about a man who believed he was dead. The psychiatrist wanted to convince him that he was not dead, so he tried using a bit of logic. He asked, "do dead men bleed?" and the guy said of course not. Then the psychiatrist poked the guy's finger with a needle and drew blood. The guy said, "Well, I'll be damned—dead men *do* bleed."

Are we sometimes like the crazy guy? Do we cling so tightly to our beliefs that we refuse to face reality? Do we feel threatened by any challenge to our cherished beliefs? My philosophy is that if someone wants to challenge something I believe—go for it! Examining my beliefs is a win-win situation: if I'm right, answering a challenge will strengthen my convictions; if I'm wrong, I *want* to change that belief. I know that *everybody*, including me, is wrong about something, and I want to find the things I'm wrong about so I can correct them.

By definition, all of us believe what we believe. In other words, we think we are right in our beliefs; otherwise we wouldn't hold those beliefs. But a wise person knows when to be open to changing his or her beliefs. Christians above all should be seekers of truth and should be humble enough to recognize when they are wrong. Just as certainty can be good or bad, so doubt can be good or bad. James warns against the kind of doubt that tosses us around and makes us unstable (1:6-8), but there is a healthy doubt that leads us to ask if we might be mistaken. We must continually ask ourselves, are we holding steadfastly to the truths of the faith, or are we clinging to manmade dogma and flawed understandings?

A devotional in *Our Daily Bread* warned against being rash in our declarations of what Scripture teaches. For example, Christians believed for centuries that the Bible taught that the earth is the center of the universe. When Galileo promoted the Copernican view that the earth moves around the sun, he was tried by the Roman Inquisition, declared "vehemently suspect of heresy," forced to recant, and consigned to house arrest.

A similar blunder was made by a bishop who was visiting the president of a college. The bishop expressed his certainty that the Bible taught that nothing new could be invented. The educator believed that the day would come when men would invent machines to fly like birds. The bishop declared, "Flight is strictly reserved for the angels, and I beg you not to repeat your suggestion lest you be guilty of blasphemy!"

The bishop was actually Milton Wright, the father of Orville and Wilbur, who only 30 years later made the first flight in a heavier-than-air machine. The devotional concludes,

> The Bible has suffered more from the unguarded tongues of its friends than from the evil barbs of its enemies! Do not rashly declare that your pet notions are "scriptural" when they are only bigoted opinions. Beware of making the bishop's blunder!

If we allow God to use our honest doubt to make us wrestle with ideas, He can bring us through to stronger convictions about His truths while keeping us humble about what we do not understand. He wants us to be willing to have our ideas challenged and charitable toward others who disagree, while resting in the certainty and assurance of faith. May He grant us the grace, humility, and wisdom to keep this balance.

> Those who have served well gain an excellent standing and great assurance in their faith in Christ Jesus (1 Tim. 3:13).

> Let us draw near to God with a sincere heart and with the full assurance that faith brings (Heb. 10:22).

"HE HIMSELF IS OUR PEACE"

Once I saw this guy on a bridge about to jump.
I said, "Don't do it!"
He said, "Nobody loves me."
I said, "God loves you. Do you believe in God?"
He said, "Yes."
I said, "Are you a Christian or a Jew?"
He said, "A Christian."
I said, "Me too! Protestant or Catholic?"
He said, "Protestant."
I said, "Me too! What franchise?"
He said, "Baptist."
I said, "Me too! Northern Baptist or Southern Baptist?"
He said, "Northern Baptist."
I said, "Me too! Northern Conservative Baptist or Northern Liberal Baptist?"
He said, "Northern Conservative Baptist."
I said, "Me too! Northern Conservative Baptist Great Lakes Region or Northern Conservative Baptist Eastern Region?"
He said, "Northern Conservative Baptist Great Lakes Region."
I said, "Me too! Northern Conservative Baptist Great Lakes Region Council of 1879 or Northern Conservative Baptist Great Lakes Region Council of 1912?"
He said, "Northern Conservative Baptist Great Lakes Region Council of 1912."
I said, "Die, heretic!" And I pushed him over.[1]

Pursuing the kind of unity Jesus prayed for in John 17 is extremely important in order to honor Him, to have healthy and joyful churches, and to present a convincing witness to the world. Christian unity does not mean agreeing with everybody or saying that all beliefs are equally valid. There are certain beliefs that are foundational to Christianity. All Christians agree on these points because they are the very ones that identify us as Christians; a person who rejects these basic tenets is not a "Christian," not because he or she is not a nice person, but because these convictions constitute the definition of "Christian."

Although some Christians take it upon themselves to define who is a Christian and who isn't, it is unwise for any one of us to make our own definition of the essentials of the faith. That was done for us very capably nearly 1700 years ago by more than two hundred bishops from around the world who came together for that purpose. The statement of faith formulated by the Council of Nicea in AD 325 embodies the essence of what it means to be a Christian. In the midst of theological controversy, they came to a consensus about the basics of the faith, and that statement is accepted by most Christians even today. Though the Nicene Creed has been translated into many different languages and the wording has been modified, the same basic statement of faith has been recited by countless Christians down through the ages.

The framers of the Nicene Creed deliberated thoughtfully about what to include as the fundamentals of the faith. They also considered carefully what *not* to include. They wisely left out those matters that are disputable, the ones that Christians can disagree on and still be Christians. They understood that unity is not dependent on being in agreement about the non-essentials. For example, the creed states that the Father made heaven and earth through the Son, but it does *not* state when and how the universe was made. It says that for our sake Jesus was crucified, he suffered death and was buried, and on the third day he rose again, but it does *not* say how we should be baptized or how we should celebrate communion/the Lord's Supper/eucharist. It says the Holy Spirit is the giver of life and should be worshiped and glorified, but it does *not* speak of spiritual gifts. It says that Jesus will come again in glory to judge the living and the dead and that we look for the resurrection of the dead and the life of the world to come, but it does not say who will be resurrected or what the world to come will be like.

It is clear that we will not have biblical unity if we all make our own determinations about what everyone has to believe and do in order to be a true Christian. We do need to be solid as a rock on the absolute truths of our faith, but we also need great wisdom to discern the difference between the essentials and the peripherals. The statement of faith of any church or Christian organization will include their denominational or organizational *distinctives*, but we need to be careful not to turn those distinctives into absolutes upon which our fellowship and unity depend. The Nicene Creed (like the shorter but similar Apostles' Creed) can give us guidance to separate the few true non-negotiables from the vastly greater number of beliefs in the gray area, where Scripture allows latitude for a variety of understandings.

Like any family, the Body of Christ does not have to agree about everything in order to be healthy. We are joined together by our birth into the family, and we grow together in unity as we respect one another and help each other follow God's will. If God could bring together into His household both Jews and Gentiles—sworn enemies who were from totally different backgrounds—then He can unite anybody:

> He himself is our peace, who has made the two one and has destroyed the barrier, the dividing wall of hostility.... His purpose was to create in himself one new man out of the two, thus making peace, and in this one body to reconcile both of them to God through the cross. (Eph. 2:14-16).

The mystery of God's will "according to his good pleasure, which he purposed in Christ" is "to bring unity to all things in heaven and on earth under Christ" (Eph. 1:9-10). The Word of God exhorts us to have unity and tells the blessings of experiencing it:

How good and pleasant it is when brothers live together in unity! (Ps. 133:1).

Make every effort to keep the unity of the Spirit through the bond of peace…. To each one of us grace has been given…to prepare God's people for works of service, so that the body of Christ may be built up until we all reach unity in the faith and in the knowledge of the Son of God and become mature, attaining to the whole measure of the fullness of Christ (Eph. 4:3, 7, 12-13).

If you have any encouragement from being united with Christ, if any comfort from his love, if any fellowship with the Spirit, if any tenderness and compassion, then make my joy complete by being like-minded, having the same love, being one in spirit and purpose. Do nothing out of selfish ambition or vain conceit, but in humility consider others better than yourselves. . . . Your attitude should be the same as that of Christ Jesus (Phil. 2:1-5).

My goal is that they may be encouraged in heart and united in love, so that they may have the full riches of complete understanding, in order that they may know the mystery of God, namely, Christ, in whom are hidden all the treasures of wisdom and knowledge (Col. 2:2-3).

Above all, our unity glorifies and pleases God, who accepts us and wants us to accept one another:

May the God who gives endurance and encouragement give you a spirit of unity among yourselves as you follow Christ, so that with one heart and mouth you may glorify the God and Father of our Lord Jesus Christ. Accept one another just as Christ accepted you, in order to bring praise to God (Rom. 15:5-7).

---

[1] Philips, Emo, *Reader's Digest*, October 2011, pp 124-125

"DON'T TOSS THE CHILDREN'S BREAD TO THE DOGS"

J esus left that place and went to the vicinity of Tyre…. As soon as she heard about him, a woman whose little daughter was possessed by an impure spirit came and fell at his feet. The woman was a Greek, born in Syrian Phoenicia. She begged Jesus to drive the demon out of her daughter.

"First let the children eat all they want," he told her, "for it is not right to take the children's bread and toss it to the dogs."

"Lord," she replied, "even the dogs under the table eat the children's crumbs."

Then he told her, "For such a reply, you may go; the demon has left your daughter."

She went home and found her child lying on the bed, and the demon gone (Mk. 7:24-30).

This incident has always troubled me. The poor woman comes to Jesus trying to get help for her little girl, and Jesus speaks scornfully to her, even insinuating that she is no more than a dog. The account in Matthew is even worse—at first He completely ignores her. Modern psychology would say that the woman now needs therapy to heal her wounded spirit, and Jesus needs lessons in how to interact with people without damaging their self-esteem!

Yet I wonder if Jesus is actually offering an opportunity for this Gentile woman's faith to shine through: He puts up an obstacle and by faith she presses on, receiving not only the answer to her prayer, but also a place in Scripture as a model of faith—remembered and respected for two thousand years.

Certainly this incident secures for her a place of honor, but maybe there's more to it. What is really going on here? What explanation is consistent with Jesus' holy character and compassionate heart and with the way He treats the poor, the outcasts, and the desperate? I now think that, far from giving the woman the brush-off, He is actually entering into a very intimate and tender moment with her. I picture Him saying to her "First let the children eat all they want, for it is not right to take the children's bread and toss it to the dogs" with a twinkle in His eye. Think about how you can be playful with someone you are close to in a way that you can't with someone who is just an acquaintance. Jesus is speaking to her with the familiarity of a close friend or family member. What He is communicating to her is, "Some people think they are the 'children' and you are just a 'dog,' but in My eyes, you and your daughter are very precious."

And *she gets it!* She is quick to respond with a witty answer of her own: "Lord, even the dogs under the table eat the children's crumbs." She recognizes that He is bantering with her, and she understands that even the "crumbs" of His power are strong enough to heal her daughter. The people around them probably overhear their conversation, but they don't get it. The woman, however, is fully engaged with Jesus in their inside joke. She realizes that she has just experienced an extraordinary connection with the Savior.

This woman's experience is unique, but it is similar to that of many others who have a personal interaction with Jesus, in the sense that each encounter is tailor-made by the Lord for that individual. In Mark alone there are many of these stories. Think of the deaf-mute man and the blind man at Bethsaida, whose stories follow the woman's. Remember the man with the unclean spirit, Peter's sick mother-in-law, and the leper in Mark 1; the paralyzed man in Mark 2; and the man with the shriveled hand in Mark 3. How about the Gadarene demoniac, the bleeding woman, the synagogue ruler with a dying daughter, the boy with an evil spirit, the rich young ruler, blind Bartimaeus, and Mary, who anoints Him in Bethany.

The other gospels record many of these stories, as well as others: the widow whose only son has died, the crippled woman who cannot straighten up, the royal official of Capernaum whose son is sick, the woman at the well in Samaria, the invalid at the pool of Bethesda, the man born blind, the woman caught in adultery, the centurion whose servant is sick, the sinful woman who anoints Jesus' feet, Nicodemus the Pharisee, Zacchaeus the tax collector, Mary Magdalene who is freed from seven evil spirits, the leper who is healed by Jesus' touch, the dying thief on the cross.

Each of these people has an unforgettable personal appointment with the Incarnate Lord. He touches each one in a unique way, especially designed by Him for that particular person. So I picture the Syrophoenician woman, a desperate mom, coming to Jesus with an urgent plea for Him to save her daughter, and leaving with a heart soaring with gratitude. Not only has her little girl been healed, but the woman herself has had a remarkable close encounter with the Lord. She has connected with Him in an exceptionally personal and special way, and her life has been transformed by His touch.

STOP WHINING!

The title of a *Christianity Today* article from the year 2000 stuck in my mind and became a mantra of mine: "Get Thou Over It!" As author Jody Vickery wrote,

We believers are the most offended, wounded, upset, shocked, thunderstruck, consternated, and (the enduring favorite) outraged group of people on the planet. Is there something in the baptismal waters that makes Christians thin-skinned? Once I even read a letter from a correspondent that began, "My wife…was disturbed." Well, pardon me. Didn't mean to disturb the Mrs.

The problem has only gotten worse since the turn of the millennium. Like our society in general, evangelicals take offense at the slightest provocation, and the proliferation of Internet comment wars has produced hordes of appalled and insulted and dismayed Christians.

Did someone challenge a cherished belief of yours? Is it worth getting so worked up about it that your relationship with him is damaged? Did someone say something to you that feels hurtful? Chances are the person didn't mean to hurt you. And even if she did, is it worth getting your panties in a wad and letting it ruin your day? Do online commenters mock your faith? It is to be expected. But does your indignation reflect the message of the gospel?

You can't control the nasty things other people say (although I don't hesitate to rebuke the ones who make the obnoxious statements). And you can't help feeling the way you feel when you are the object of rude, demeaning, or offensive words. But *you can choose* not to take offense, not to retaliate, and not to brood over the insult in such a way that it makes you simmer inside. And if you need a tactile reminder, slip a Q-Tip into your pocket and touch it when you are feeling offended. Let it remind you to "**Q**uit **T**aking **I**t **P**ersonally!"

And while you're getting over "it," try to get over yourself. In the words of Tony Gaskins, "The biggest hurdle in life is getting over yourself. Once you get over yourself, you can get anywhere." Humor can be a good tool to defuse a situation; making fun of yourself takes the punch out of someone else's attempt to ridicule you.

So if your outrage is a reaction to a personal affront, you need to suck it up and let it go or deal with it in a constructive way. If it is righteous anger, find a way to channel it for good. As Jody Vickery says, "You could fuel enough furnaces for a Minnesota winter if scientists could find a way to convert all that religious indignation into a useful energy source." When you feel the dismay or resentment rising, let it be a cue to seek a positive response and to call to mind this mantra: Get thou over it!

WHO'S THE BEST?

When my son Andy was in college in South Carolina, he called me up one day and said, "Hey Mom, my roommates and I are having a competition to see whose mother is the best baker. Could you send some banana bread and poppy seed cake?" It was a thinly disguised request for a care package, but it worked. I have to confess that part of the reason why it worked was because of my own pride and competitiveness. Lurking at the back of my mind was the idea, "I bet *my* goodies are better than the other mothers'."

The disciples had the same problem. One day James and John came to Jesus and said, "We want you to give *us* the best seats in your kingdom." The other disciples were indignant because *they* wanted the best seats for themselves.

So Jesus had to call them all together to try to straighten them out and make them understand Kingdom values. As in so many areas, He took the values of the world and completely flipped them on their heads:

> You know that those who are regarded as rulers of the Gentiles lord it over them, and their high officials exercise authority over them. *Not so with you.* Instead, whoever wants to become great among you must be your servant, and whoever wants to be first must be slave of all. For even the Son of Man did not come to be served, but to serve, and to give his life as a ransom for many (Mark 10:42-45).

True leadership is **servant leadership**—leading the way in serving. It's not about exercising power over others but about building them up. It's not about being better than others but about growing together. It's not about imposing your will but about guiding people to cooperate for the good of all.

How can we develop the quality of servant leadership? By following the model of Jesus Christ:

> Do nothing out of selfish ambition or vain conceit. Rather, in humility value others above yourselves, not looking to your own interests but each of you to the interests of the others. In your relationships with one another, have the same mindset as Christ Jesus: Who, being in very nature God, did not consider equality with God something to be used to his own advantage; rather, he made himself nothing by taking the very nature of a servant, being made in human likeness. And being found in appearance as a man, he humbled himself by becoming obedient to death—even death on a cross! (Phil. 2:3-8)

"THE SPIRIT CATCHES YOU AND YOU FALL DOWN"

In the early 1980s, the Lee family—husband Nao Kao, wife Foua, and their six surviving children—escaped from the Communist regime in Laos and made their way to California's Central Valley, where many other Hmong refugees had settled. In 1982, their daughter Lia was born. Unlike her parents and twelve brothers and sisters before her, who were delivered into their mother's hands as she squatted alone and silently over a dirt floor, Lia was born in a modern hospital, where her mother lay on her back on a steel table and gave birth to her baby into the hands of a male doctor.

At the age of three months, Lia started having severe epileptic seizures. Her parents would take her to the hospital to get help, but they did not speak English and they did not trust the doctors or understand the complicated treatment she received. Anne Fadiman's book *The Spirit Catches You and You Fall Down: A Hmong Child, Her American Doctors, and the Collision of Two Cultures*[1] chronicles the Lees' confusing and often terrifying odyssey through the American medical system.

The book highlights the enormous differences between the Hmong mindset and the American mindset. Even the title speaks of a fundamental difference in the way epilepsy is viewed in the two cultures; while American medicine sees it as a physical disorder caused by abnormal neuronal activity, Hmong people attribute it to spiritual forces. The book is sensitively written, with a balanced presentation of the perspectives and perceptions of both cultures. The author expressed her thanks to the Lee family, "who changed my whole way of looking at the world when they welcomed me into their home, their daily lives, and their rich culture" (page 329). If you read her book with an honest, open mind, it will make you rethink your own assumptions about what constitutes good medical care, what makes a healthy family, what it means to be a good parent, and even what is the nature of truth.

Having been in an intercultural marriage for more than 40 years, I am well aware of the fact that huge misunderstandings in a relationship can be generated by our cultural biases. The partners may not be consciously aware of the presuppositions and expectations they bring into the marriage, but their words and actions spring from the basic beliefs they hold. The less they have in common, the greater the potential for misunderstanding and conflict, and for comedy but also tragedy.

Missionaries going into a foreign culture also need to understand this phenomenon. I think missionaries would do well to read *The Spirit Catches You and You Fall Down*. Not that every foreign culture is like the Hmong, but this book alerts you to the fact that vast differences do exist between cultures. It helps you get into the mind and heart of someone who thinks and feels and experiences life very differently. As the author asks, "If you can't see that your own culture has its own set of interests, emotions, and biases, how can you expect to deal successfully with someone else's culture?" (page 261). Those who want to minister to the whole person—body, soul, and spirit—will be most effective if they can truly walk in another person's shoes and understand how the other person thinks and feels.

God Himself is the model for entering fully into the life of others. He could have stayed in heaven, but He chose to become flesh and dwell among us and experience human existence fully. He understands us not only because of His omniscience, but also because He humbled Himself and became a human being, taking on our limitations and seeing life through our eyes. May He open our eyes to understand others and to know how to communicate to them the good news of His coming to earth to live and die for us.

Spoiler Alert: If you want to read the book yourself and find out what happened to Lia Lee, stop here! Otherwise, read on to learn the end of the story.

Despite the medical community's best efforts to help Lia, her seizures became increasingly frequent and severe. At one point, doctors and social workers decided that her parents were not being compliant enough with the prescribed treatment (which in the parents' view was making her worse), and Lia was removed from her home and placed in a foster home for nine months, to the unbearable anguish of her family.

At the age of four, Lia suffered a grand mal seizure that the doctors were unable to control. She was left in a persistent vegetative state, and there was nothing more that American medicine could do for her, so she was sent home to die, which doctors believed would happen imminently. But in the loving care of her family, Lia lived for 26 more years, finally passing away in August 2012 at the age of 30. Throughout that time, Lia's family practiced their traditional rituals, which are extremely suspect in the eyes of the American medical establishment, but they treated her with utmost dignity and nurtured her with tender compassion.

So what was the "right" way to treat a patient like Lia? I hope you come away with the realization that there are no easy, cut-and-dried answers. I hope you will also have a greater appreciation of the richness of different cultures and will make a concerted effort to understand others who may be very different from you.

---

[1] Fadiman, Anne. *The Spirit Catches You and You Fall Down*. Farrar, Straus, and Giroux. 1997.

"DO NOT REPAY EVIL FOR EVIL"

In chapter 3 of his first epistle, Peter discusses husband-wife relationships and then gives exhortations about relationships in general. Paul and James give additional instructions about how to treat others, particularly with our words. I would like to share these passages without commentary; they need no exegesis—only obedience. I will quote them from *The Message*, in hopes that a different translation might help us to see them with fresh eyes and to be open to being humbled and convicted by the Holy Spirit.

> Summing up: Be agreeable, be sympathetic, be loving, be compassionate, be humble. That goes for all of you, no exceptions. No retaliation. No sharp-tongued sarcasm. Instead, bless—that's your job, to bless. You'll be a blessing and also get a blessing.

> Whoever wants to embrace life
>   and see the day fill up with good,
> Here's what you do:
>   Say nothing evil or hurtful;
> Snub evil and cultivate good;
>   run after peace for all you're worth.
> God looks on all this with approval,
>   listening and responding well to what he's asked;
> But he turns his back
>   on those who do evil things (1 Pet. 3:8-12).

> Watch the way you talk. Let nothing foul or dirty come out of your mouth. Say only what helps, each word a gift (Eph. 4:29).

This is scary: You can tame a tiger, but you can't tame a tongue—it's never been done. The tongue runs wild, a wanton killer. With our tongues we bless God our Father; with the same tongues we curse the very men and women he made in his image. Curses and blessings out of the same mouth! My friends, this can't go on (Js. 3:7-10).

Real wisdom, God's wisdom, begins with a holy life and is characterized by getting along with others. It is gentle and reasonable, overflowing with mercy and blessings, not hot one day and cold the next, not two-faced. You can develop a healthy, robust community that lives right with God and enjoy its results *only* if you do the hard work of getting along with each other, treating each other with dignity and honor (Js. 3:17-18).

The Message version of Jesus' words in Luke 6 is worth quoting in its entirety:

"To you who are ready for the truth, I say this: Love your enemies. Let them bring out the best in you, not the worst. When someone gives you a hard time, respond with the energies of prayer for that person. If someone slaps you in the face, stand there and take it. If someone grabs your shirt, giftwrap your best coat and make a present of it. If someone takes unfair advantage of you, use the occasion to practice the servant life. No more tit-for-tat stuff. Live generously.

"Here is a simple rule of thumb for behavior: Ask yourself what you want people to do for you; then grab the initiative and do it for *them*! If you only love the lovable, do you expect a pat on the back? Run-of-the-mill sinners do that. If you only help those who help you, do you expect a medal? Garden-variety sinners do that. If you only give for what you hope to get out of it, do you think that's charity? The stingiest of pawnbrokers does that.

"I tell you, love your enemies. Help and give without expecting a return. You'll never—I promise—regret it. Live out this God-created identity the way our Father lives toward us, generously and graciously, even when we're at our worst. Our Father is kind; you be kind.

"Don't pick on people, jump on their failures, criticize their faults—unless, of course, you want the same treatment. Don't condemn those who are down; that hardness can boomerang. Be easy on people; you'll find life a lot easier. Give away your life; you'll find life given back, but not merely given back—given back with bonus and blessing. Giving, not getting, is the way. Generosity begets generosity....

"It's easy to see a smudge on your neighbor's face and be oblivious to the ugly sneer on your own. Do you have the nerve to say, 'Let me wash your face for you,' when your own face is distorted by contempt? It's this I-know-better-than-you mentality again, playing a holier-than-thou part instead of just living your own part. Wipe that ugly sneer off your own face and you might be fit to offer a washcloth to your neighbor" (Lk. 6:27-42).

For those times we have been guilty of returning insult for insult, let us ask forgiveness. And if we do it in the future, let us be willing for others to bring it to our attention. And I urge us all to check all our communication against these exhortations from Jesus, Peter, Paul, and James.

"JESUS LOVES ME, THIS I KNOW!"

Jesus loves me! This I know,
For the Bible tells me so.
Susan Warner, 1860

Some Christians are able to accept the simple declaration of God's love: "Jesus loves me! This I know, for the Bible tells me so." But others struggle to believe they are loved by a God they can't even see, especially when His earthly representatives fail to show love.

Sometimes it may indeed seem that God's love is conditional or even fickle—that He keeps His covenant of love *if* we love Him and obey Him and do what is right. And we can never be sure we have obeyed Him well enough. Yet the Bible speaks over and over of God's unconditional love—that He IS love regardless of who we are (1 Jn. 4:8).

The Old Testament declares God's "unfailing love" or "steadfast love" dozens of times. Many times God is said to be "a compassionate and gracious God, slow to anger, abounding in love and faithfulness." Psalm 107 repeatedly says, "Let them give thanks to the Lord for his unfailing love and his wonderful deeds for mankind." "His love endures forever" is affirmed five times in Psalm 118 and 26 times in Psalm 136. Jeremiah says His compassions never fail (Lam. 3:22), His love is everlasting, and His kindness is unfailing (Jer. 31:3).

The New Testament reaffirms that God loves us even though we are fallen sinners.

God demonstrates his own love for us in this: While we were still sinners, Christ died for us (Rom. 5:8).

Because of his great love for us, God, who is rich in mercy, made us alive with Christ even when we were dead in transgressions" (Eph. 2:4-5).

If God's love for us depends on something we do, even if the "something" is just "accepting" His love or "receiving" Christ or "having faith" or "trusting Jesus," then His love is conditional and we can never be sure we have met the conditions. The words of "Jesus Loves Me" get it right:

Jesus loves me when I'm good,
When I do the things I should,
Jesus loves me when I'm bad,
Though it makes Him very sad.

Neither is His love restricted to certain categories of people. God IS love, so I can be confident that He will never waver in His love for anyone, including me. As Charles Wesley put it, "Jesus, Thou art all compassion, pure unbounded love Thou art." Knowing that God's love is not limited is the sure foundation for solid faith in Him.

Paul had trouble expressing the extent of God's multi-dimensional love, but he wanted us to grasp how vast it is so that we can have unshakeable faith:

Neither death nor life, neither angels nor demons, neither the present nor the future, nor any powers, neither height nor depth, nor anything else in all creation, will be able to separate us from the love of God that is in Christ Jesus our Lord (Rom. 8:38-39).

I pray that out of his glorious riches he may strengthen you with power through his Spirit in your inner being, so that Christ may dwell in your hearts through faith. And I pray that you, being rooted and established in love, may have power, together with all the Lord's holy people, to grasp how wide and long and high and deep is the love of Christ, and to know this love that surpasses knowledge—that you may be filled to the measure of all the fullness of God (Eph. 3:16-19).

Let the words of these hymns sink deep into your heart and grip you with the immensity of God's love. Here is a God you can trust fully because He is sovereign, He is wise, and He is love!

O the deep, deep love of Jesus, vast, unmeasured,
    boundless, free!
Rolling as a mighty ocean in its fullness over me!
Underneath me, all around me, is the current of Thy
    love
Leading onward, leading homeward to Thy glorious
    rest above!

O the deep, deep love of Jesus, spread His praise
    from shore to shore!
How He loveth, ever loveth, changeth never,
    nevermore!
How He watches o'er His loved ones, died to call
    them all His own;
How for them He intercedeth, watcheth o'er them
    from the throne!
                              S. Trevor Francis, 1875

The love of God is greater far
Than tongue or pen can ever tell;
It goes beyond the highest star,
And reaches to the lowest hell;
The guilty pair, bowed down with care,
God gave His Son to win;
His erring child He reconciled,
And pardoned from his sin.

O love of God, how rich and pure!
How measureless and strong!
It shall forevermore endure
The saints' and angels' song.

When years of time shall pass away,
And earthly thrones and kingdoms fall,

When men, who here refuse to pray,
On rocks and hills and mountains call,
God's love so sure, shall still endure,
All measureless and strong;
Redeeming grace to Adam's race—
The saints' and angels' song.

Could we with ink the ocean fill,
And were the skies of parchment made,
Were every stalk on earth a quill,
And every man a scribe by trade,
To write the love of God above,
Would drain the ocean dry.
Nor could the scroll contain the whole,
Though stretched from sky to sky.

Frederick M. Lehman, 1917

SKIP THE CHEEZ WHIZ

" "Fruitful Words" (page 37) was about the fruit of
the Spirit as expressed in our words. Here we'll
talk about vegetables. There's a lesson in vegetables (although I've never heard of the vegetables of the Spirit).

Colossians 2 speaks of the problem with human reason.
Paul says,

> See to it that no one takes you captive by philosophy
> and empty deceit, according to human tradition,…
> not according to Christ (2:8).

Human philosophy can take different forms, and we need
to be alert not just to the obvious dangers of human reason
but also to the more subtle ones. Some human philosophy
involves outright rejection of God and His truth, which is not
hard to identify. A greater problem for Bible-believing Christians is accepting Scripture as the Word of God but then
allowing biblical truth to be encrusted over with layers of
human reason and speculation. Let me explain.

I'm all for systematic theology—taking revealed truth and
trying to put it all together into a coherent whole. But as we
develop a complex system that tries to explain it all, we run
the risk of losing sight of the simple truths of the gospel. Paul
does want us to have "full assurance of understanding and
the knowledge of God's mystery" (Col. 2:2), but the "mystery"
is not some esoteric philosophy that can be understood only
by a select few. The "mystery" is Jesus Himself, and the
"knowledge" is knowing Him, "in whom are hidden all the
treasures of wisdom and knowledge" (Col. 2:3).

Human reason can suck the life right out of the truths of Scripture. Systems of theology can become deadly rather than life-giving. I'm reminded of a passage from a book by Harriet Beecher Stowe[1] that describes the theological systems that were prevalent in Puritan New England:

> But it is to be conceded that these systems, so admirable in relation to the energy, earnestness, and acuteness of their authors, when received as absolute truth, and as a basis of actual life, had, on minds of a certain class, the effect of a slow poison, producing life habits of morbid action very different from any which ever followed the simple reading of the Bible. They differ from the New Testament as the living embrace of a friend does from his lifeless body, mapped out under the knife of the anatomical demonstrator; every nerve and muscle is there, but to a sensitive spirit there is the very chill of death in the analysis.
>
> All systems that deal with the infinite are, besides, exposed to danger from small, unsuspected admixtures of human error, which become deadly when carried to such vast results. The smallest speck of earth's dust, in the focus of an infinite lens, appears magnified among the heavenly orbs as a frightful monster.

I picture the truths of Scripture as being like a beautiful basket of fresh vegetables—colorful, flavorful, delicious, nutritious. Some people just reject vegetables altogether. But is it any better to cook them to death and smother them with Cheez Whiz? They are no longer life-giving—the color and the flavor and the nourishment are gone. Could it be that we lose sight of the simple and beautiful truths of Scripture when we build elaborate systems of theology based on human wisdom? And even a small "admixture of human error" in our systems of theology can become "a frightful monster."

One of the characters in C. S. Lewis's *The Great Divorce*[2] puts it this way:

There have been men before now who got so interested in proving the existence of God that they came to care nothing for God Himself.... There have been some who were so occupied in spreading Christianity that they never gave a thought to Christ.... Did ye never know a lover of books that with all his first editions and signed copies had lost the power to read them? Or an organiser of charities that had lost all love for the poor? It is the subtlest of all the snares.

Another character speaks of the artist who gets so caught up in his own art that he forgets the One who created him and gave him the gift of creativity:

Every poet and musician and artist, but for Grace, is drawn away from love of the thing he tells, to love of the telling till, down in Deep Hell, they cannot be interested in God at all but only in what they say about Him.

What doctrines constitute the basic, non-negotiable principles of our faith—the simple truths that we must not allow to get buried under our theologizing? Here is my Sunday-school version of systematic theology:[3]

1) God created the world.

2) God loves the world.

3) The world rebelled against God.

4) God purposed to save the world.

5) The whole fullness of God dwells in His Son, who is the Savior of the world.

6) God sent His Son into the world to save the world.

7) In the fullness of time, Jesus will return and God will fulfill His purpose to restore His creation in Christ.

Have we strayed from these simple truths and become entangled in wrangling about doctrine? Are we so intent on proving a theological point that we forget the big picture of what God is doing and how He wants us to live? Then it's time to get back to pure and simple faith in the Savior. For all the doctrinal treatises he wrote, Paul knew what was most important:

> And I, when I came to you, brothers, did not come proclaiming to you the testimony of God with lofty speech or wisdom. For I decided to know nothing among you except Jesus Christ and him crucified (1 Cor. 2:1).

From the beginning Satan has been trying to seduce us, and one way is by turning us away from simple truth and sincere faith:

> But I am afraid that as the serpent deceived Eve by his cunning, your thoughts will be led astray from a sincere and pure devotion to Christ (2 Cor. 11:3).

If you find yourself being caught up in human philosophizing and theologizing, stop and return to sincere and pure devotion to the Savior!

---

[1] Stowe, Harriet Beecher, *The Minister's Wooing.* 1859.

[2] Lewis, C.S., *The Great Divorce.* 1945.

[3] Scripture references:
1) Gen. 1:1; Col. 1:16
2) Jn. 3:16; Rom. 5:8
3) Jn. 3:19; Eph. 2:2
4) Jn. 3:17; Jn. 12:47
5) Col. 2:9; Col. 1:19-20
6) 1 Jn. 2:2; 1 Jn. 4:14
7) Eph. 1:9-10; Col. 1:19-20

THE MINISTER'S WOOING

Many years ago, I read *Uncle Tom's Cabin* and was so moved that I read another novel by Harriet Beecher Stowe, *The Minister's Wooing*, set in eighteenth-century New England. Mrs. Marvyn's son Jim, who was not a professing believer, has been lost at sea, and Mrs. Marvyn is wracked with grief and despair to the point where she abandons her faith. Her young friend Mary is at a loss to help her, and for all their lofty ideas, the theologians, like Dr. Samuel Hopkins, have nothing to offer the grief-stricken mother. But in comes Candace, her old black maid, who "talks gospel" to her. Unlike the theologians, Candace gets it! Her words have often ministered to me; I photocopied the chapter with Candace's words and pull it out when I need to be reminded who Jesus really is and how much God loves us. Compare a human system of theology to the pure and simple gospel!

As Harriet Beecher Stowe explains, the folks of Puritan New England examined, discussed, and practiced their faith with an intensity seldom seen:

> Never was there a community where the roots of common life shot down so deeply, and were so intensely grappled around things sublime and eternal.... Living an intense, earnest, practical life, mostly tilling the earth with their own hands, they yet carried on the most startling and original religious investigations.

They took on the monumental task of trying to explain how such evil can exist in a world created and ruled by a good God:

The task they proposed to themselves was that of reconciling the most tremendous facts of sin and evil, present and eternal, with those conceptions of Infinite Power and Benevolence which their own strong and generous natures enabled them so vividly to realize.

And their beliefs were not mere abstract reflections but rather the sturdy basis of their everyday lives:

No man or woman accepted any theory or speculation simply as theory or speculation; all was profoundly real and vital, a foundation on which actual life was based with intensest earnestness.

Yet for all their intensity and devotion, few experienced the joy of the Lord:

The views of human existence which resulted from this course of training were gloomy enough to oppress any heart which did not rise above them by triumphant faith or sink below them by brutish insensibility.

Believing that God was infinitely wise and powerful but that only "the merest fragment of mankind" would escape His condemnation meant that

tremendous internal conflict and agitation were all the while working in every bosom…. While strong spirits walked, palm-crowned, with victorious hymns, along these sublime paths, feebler and more sensitive ones lay along the track, bleeding away in lifelong despair.

Mrs. Marvyn was one of those souls who lived "under a cloud of religious gloom." When she lost her son, she suffered a complete collapse. In her agony she cried out,

Life seems to me the most tremendous doom that can be inflicted on a helpless being! What had we done, that it should be sent upon us? Why were we made to love so, to hope so, our hearts so full of feeling, and all the laws of Nature marching over us, never stopping for our agony? Why, we can suffer so in this life that we had better never have been born!

No one could comfort Mrs. Marvyn—until Candace burst into the room.

"Lor' bress ye, Squire Marvyn, we won't hab her goin' on dis yer way," she said. "Do talk gospel to her, can't ye—ef you can't, I will.

"Come, ye poor little lamb," she said, walking straight up to Mrs. Marvyn, "come to ole Candace!" and with that she gathered the pale form to her bosom, and sat down and began rocking her, as if she had been a babe. "Honey, darlin', ye ain't right, dar's a dreful mistake somewhar," she said. "Why, de Lord ain't like what ye tink. He loves ye, honey! Why, jes' feel how *I* loves ye, poor ole black Candace, an' I ain't better 'n Him as made me! Who was it wore de crown o' thorns, lamb? Who was it sweat great drops o' blood? who was it said, 'Father, forgive dem'? Say, honey! wasn't it de Lord dat made ye? Dar, dar, now ye'r' cryin'! cry away, and ease yer poor little heart! He died for Mass'r Jim, loved him and died for him, jes' give up his sweet, precious body and soul for him on de cross! Laws, jes' leave him in Jesus's hands! Why, honey, dar's de very print o' de nails in his hands now!"

The flood-gates were rent; and healing sobs and tears shook the frail form, as a faded lily shakes under the soft rains of summer. All in the room wept together.

"Now, honey," said Candace, after a pause of some minutes, "I knows our Doctor's a mighty good man, an' larned, an' in fair weather I hain't no 'bjection to yer hearin' all about dese yer great an' mighty tings he's got to say. But, honey, dey won't do for you now; sick folks mus' n't hab strong meat; an' times like dese, dar jest ain't but one ting to come to, an' dat ar's Jesus. Jes' come right down to whar poor ole black

Candace has to stay allers, it's a good place, darlin'! Look right at Jesus. Tell ye, honey, ye can't live no other way now. Don't ye 'member how He looked on his mother, when she stood faintin' an' tremblin' under de cross, jes' like you? He knows all about mothers' hearts; He won't break yours. It was jes' 'cause He know'd we'd come into straits like dis yer, dat He went through all dese tings, Him, de Lord o' Glory! Is dis Him you was a-talkin' about? Him you can't love? Look at Him, an' see ef you can't. Look an' see what He is! Don't ask no questions, and don't go to no reasonin's, jes' look at Him, hangin' dar, so sweet and patient, on de cross! All dey could do couldn't stop his lovin' 'em; He prayed for 'em wid all de breath He had. Dar's a God you can love, ain't dar? Candace loves Him, poor, ole, foolish, black, wicked Candace, and she knows He loves her," and here Candace broke down into torrents of weeping.

They laid the mother, faint and weary, on her bed, and beneath the shadow of that suffering cross came down a healing sleep on those weary eyelids.

Let Candace's words sink into your soul and minister to you as they did to Mrs. Marvyn.

JESUS: A FRUITFUL AND UNFRENZIED LIFE

L et me paint a little picture; maybe some of you can relate:

Alarm rings.
Hit snooze button.
Ten minutes later, hit snooze button one more time.
Another ten minutes, stumble out of bed.
Take a quick shower.
Get dressed and put on make-up.
Grab a cup of coffee.
Get kid 1 out of bed.
Send husband off with a kiss and a bagel.
Rummage in the hamper to find semi-clean socks.
Get kid 2 up.
Find missing shoe.
Feed kids breakfast.
Eat last three bites of kid 1's soggy cereal.
Drink last inch of kid 2's orange juice.
Pack a bag lunch for one kid and scrape together
     lunch money for the other.
Make kids collect school stuff and brush their teeth.
Send kid 1 off to the bus.
Make kid 2 walk the dog.
Take kid 2 to school, go to work, hoping your boss
     won't notice that you're late.
Put out fires at work, eat lunch at your desk.

Fly home to meet kids.
Give them a snack.
Drive to soccer.
Come home and start supper.
Pick up at soccer, drive to piano lesson.
Pick up at piano lesson.
Come home and feed family.
Clean up kitchen.
Help with homework.
Make sure kids take a bath and brush their teeth.
Tuck them in.
Throw in a load of laundry so you'll have clean socks
    the next morning.

This scenario may be familiar to young moms. For people who are not married or do not have children, the busyness takes different forms. And as we move through different stages and seasons of our lives, the activities change. Or perhaps you are at a place in your life where you find yourself a bit at loose ends, with time on your hands. You don't know quite what to do with your time, so you go from one thing to another, but at the end of the day, you're not quite sure where your day went.

There can be a lot of busyness and activity in our lives, but only if we have a firm foundation and a focus will our lives be truly fruitful. Jesus faced more stress than we ever will, but He was never stressed out. How did He maintain His composure and keep pursuing God's will in the face of tremendous obstacles? The gospel of Luke gives some insight into His equanimity and sense of purpose. Luke's description of Jesus in chapter 4 shows how to live a life that is full but never frantic or frenzied, always focused and fruitful.

A Time to Be Tested (1-12)

The experience that was foundational to Jesus' whole ministry was His time in the wilderness. He was led *by the Spirit* (v. 1) in the desert, where He was tempted *by the devil* (v. 2). The same experience can be used by Satan to tempt in order to destroy or by God to test in order to build. Whenever we feel tempted or tormented by Satan, God has not abandoned us. On the contrary, we can have confidence that God is able to use the experience even more powerfully for good.

Satan tempted Jesus just as he tempts us—with lies and half-truths. Jesus countered Satan's lies with God's truth. He was full of the Holy Spirit (4:1)—the Spirit of truth—who led Him into all truth and enabled Him to recognize Satan's lies and lures. Jesus was ready to resist temptation because He knew Scripture. How did He know the Word so well? You might think, "Jesus was God, so He knew the Scriptures automatically." It is true that as a member of the Trinity, Jesus was instrumental in writing the Scriptures, along with the Father and the Holy Spirit. In fact, He *is* the Word. But it was not because of His omniscience or His deity that Jesus knew the Scriptures; as a human, He had to *learn* the Scriptures, just as we do. He had to *grow* in wisdom (Luke 2:52). How did He get the Word into His heart and know how to use it?

He listened to Bible stories and readings.
He spent time in the temple (Luke 2:49) and the synagogue ("His custom"—Luke 4:16).
He sang psalms and hymns.
He asked questions, He learned from teachers of the Word, and He discussed the Scriptures with others (Luke 2:46).
He studied on His own.
He sought wisdom from the Father (Luke 4:42).
He memorized Scripture (Luke 4:3-12).

As we learn the Word, we get better at knowing when we are being tempted to take something good in the wrong way, like the bread (Luke 4:2-4). We will be able to distinguish between a test of our faith, which is a good thing, and the temptation to put God to the test (Luke 4:9-12). We will know when we are being tempted to take for ourselves what does not belong to us—or what *will* belong to us but not yet (Luke 4:5-8).

Jesus always awaited God's timing for whatever He was to do. Satan offered to let Him rule the kingdoms of the world, but Jesus knew that His time to rule had not yet come. God often calls His people to wait and trust Him. What might God be asking you to wait for?

A Time to Be Ministered To (13)

Jesus knew, as Solomon says in Ecclesiastes, that "there is a time for everything, and a season for every activity under heaven" (3:1). Once the time of testing was over, the devil left Him and angels ministered to Him. Interspersed with the times of trial, God gives us seasons of refreshment that are to be accepted and enjoyed gratefully. These times of renewal help prepare us for Satan's next assault, for he *will* be back, as Luke says, at "an opportune time" (4:13).

A Time to Be Loved (14-22)

As soon as Jesus returned to Galilee from His time in the desert, He faced another test: the wild extremes of the people's attitudes toward Him. At first, He was adored. Everyone praised Him (4:15), they listened to His teaching (4:15-21), they spoke well of Him (4:22), and they were amazed at His gracious words (4:22).

A Time to Be Hated (23-30)

This adoration, however, quickly turned to rage and even murderous intentions. When Jesus' words pleased the people, they admired and loved Him. But as soon as He dared to speak the truth about their spiritual condition, they became furious at Him. They drove Him out of town and tried to throw Him off a cliff. If it had been His time to die, He would have accepted it in submission to the Father. But it wasn't time, so the Father made a way out for Him. He never became panic-stricken; "He walked right through the crowd and went on His way" (4:30).

Do you ever become confused or anxious when people are fickle in their feelings toward you? Do you have trouble handling criticism and rejection—or handling praise? Jesus was able to handle both the adoration and the opposition. He knew how to be humble, and He knew that His worth did not come from people's attitudes toward Him. He also knew that He did not have to please everyone; there was only one person He needed to please: His Father.

A Time to Minister (31-44)

From verse 31 until the end of the chapter, we have what appears to be a single day in the life of Jesus. If you had looked at Jesus while He was in the wilderness, you might not have thought He was very busy: no people to minister to, no meetings to attend, no cooking to do. In contrast, on this day, He was *very* busy by any standard. How did He handle all the demands on His time?

If you're anything like me, life often feels crazy: too much to do, not enough time, and even if you make lists and schedules, your day can go haywire with the intrusion of the unexpected. In contrast, although Jesus was extremely busy, you never get the sense that He was going crazy. On this day in Capernaum, He taught the people in the synagogue, He confronted demons, and He healed people late into the night. Where did He get the strength? How did He stay focused and not get frazzled?

One key is found in the first verse of this chapter and throughout the chapter: Jesus was "full of the Holy Spirit"; He was "led by the Spirit" (4:1). He returned to Galilee "in the power of the Spirit" (4:14) In reading from Isaiah, He said of Himself, "The Spirit of the Lord is on me" (4:18). In Romans, Paul elaborates on what it means to live "according to the Spirit." It means to have your "mind set on what the Spirit desires" (Romans 8:5), to be "controlled by the Spirit" (8:6, 9), to have "the Spirit of him who raised Jesus from the dead living in you" (8:11).

So what does this look like in terms of our daily activities? Jesus allowed the Father to set up appointments for Him, and then He just kept the appointments the Father had made. He didn't let Himself get pulled every which way by the demands of the urgent. He didn't have to stress about being torn by competing needs, because the Father would not ask Him to do more than what He gave ability to do. He didn't have to worry about something not getting done, because if it was not on the Father's agenda, it was not to be done that day. So He taught in the synagogue and then ministered to individuals—casting out evil spirits, healing Simon's mother-in-law, laying hands on each person who came to Him. He spent just the right amount of time with each one, neither lingering too long nor rushing off. Not everyone in Capernaum was healed that night, but Jesus completed everything the Father had given Him to do. Similarly, if we look to God for His agenda, we can have a sense of calm and purpose, even in the midst of busyness.

A Time to Be Alone with the Father

At the very end of this chapter is another clue as to where Jesus received His strength and wisdom. Verse 42 says, "At daybreak Jesus went out to a solitary place." The parallel passage in Mark tells why He went there: "Very early in the morning, while it was still dark, Jesus got up, left the house, and went off to a solitary place, where he prayed" (Mark 1:35). If Jesus got up at the crack of dawn for prayer after such a busy day, you can be sure that He did it *every* day. And if He needed to do it, how much more do *we* need to do it? This time of fellowship with the Father gave Him strength and peace. He may have received from the Father an outline of what the day would look like, to be filled in as God brought people and circumstances across His path. Being with God the Father and being filled with the Holy Spirit set the tone for the day and showed Him how to live that day according to God's will.

Summary

To summarize, here are some principles Jesus followed:

1) He was led by the Spirit (1, 14, 18).
2) He knew God's Word (3-12).

3) He was not swayed by people's opinions (14-30).
4) He let the Father make His appointments (31-44).
5) He spent time with the Father (42).

Philippians 2 shows how we can live like Jesus: "Let this mind be in you, which was also in Christ Jesus" or "Your attitude should be the same as that of Christ Jesus" (2:5). This idea is also captured in Kate B. Wilkinson's hymn "May the Mind of Christ, My Savior." May we have His mind so we can be focused and fruitful, never frantic or frenzied.

May the mind of Christ, my Savior,   *Christ's mind*
Live in me from day to day,
By His love and power controlling
All I do and say.

May the Word of God dwell richly   *God's Word*
In my heart from hour to hour,
So that all may see I triumph
Only through His power.

May the peace of God, my Father,   *The Father's peace*
Rule my life in everything,
That I may be calm to comfort
Sick and sorrowing.

May the love of Jesus fill me,   *Jesus' love*
As the waters fill the sea;
Him exalting, self abasing,
This is victory.

May His Spirit rest upon me   *The Holy Spirit*
As I seek the lost to win,
And may they forget the channel,
Seeing only Him.

"NOBODY CARES
HOW MUCH YOU KNOW...

...until they know how much you care."[1] This statement from a Bible study on 2 Peter caught my attention. Peter is coming to the end of his life, and he wants to transmit to his readers as much knowledge as he can.

> I will always remind you of these things, even though you know them and are firmly established in the truth you now have. I think it is right to refresh your memory as long as I live,.... And I will make every effort to see that after my departure you will always be able to remember these things (2 Pet. 1:12-15).

But he understands that knowledge alone is not what really counts. What really matters is that lives be transformed. Peter wants his readers to see how much God has transformed him and how much he cares about them, so that they will be receptive to his message and in turn will be open to allowing God to transform them.

Do you have knowledge you want to impart? Whether you are a parent, pastor, teacher, boss, writer, or friend, you have knowledge that you want to communicate to others. If you want them to receive it, let them know how much you care about them. You may be intellectually brilliant or theologically astute, but if you come across as arrogant, callous, or uncaring, your words will fall on deaf ears.

Nick and Sheila Rowe understand this principle and apply it in their ministry. Both are highly educated (she holds a Master's degree in Counseling Psychology and he has a Ph.D.

in history), but their goal is not to impress people with their knowledge. Rather, they seek to develop authentic Christian community and genuine relationships with people in order to get to know their stories and minister to them in a very personal way. No one is unimportant; each person, no matter how broken, has worth. They practice what Paul Young applies in his ministry when he says, "there is no person or moment more important to me than the person before whom I stand at this moment."

Sheila does counseling for individuals, couples, and groups to bring about healing and to help people understand their identity and find God's purpose for their lives. Nick leads initiatives "to promote Mediation, Conflict Resolution, Healing and Reconciliation across gender, race and ethnic lines." One hallmark of their ministry is the great diversity of their team and of the people they serve. Their goal is to make Ephesians 2:14 a reality: **"For He Himself is our peace, who has made the two groups one and has destroyed the barrier, the dividing wall of hostility."** The testimony of a woman from Ireland speaks to the effectiveness of their work in giving a glimpse of the king-

Sheila Wise Rowe

Nicholas Rowe

dom of God: "Your ability to teach, share your story and also empathize with others has not only blessed me, it has demonstrated the Father's kingdom in a new way."

The Rowes' work takes them into all kinds of situations, sometimes dangerous ones. During their first meeting with one group, a young man stumbled into the church with a gunshot wound and collapsed in the foyer, the victim of a drive-by shooting. They not only ministered to the people through that trauma but also returned to continue the work God had started.

Besides the U.S., the Rowes have served in Zambia, Thailand, France, Lesotho, and most recently ten years in South Africa, where they had a ministry of reconciliation. One person whose life was transformed was a woman who lived in the catacombs under a cemetery with her two nieces. Her sister had died of AIDS, leaving the children with her. She had spent time in jail and was a lost, broken person, but she and the girls were taken in and shown the love of Christ. She learned to deal with the anger and hurt caused by the abuse and loss in her life, and she became a new person. She joined the staff of a program for handicapped people, and the girls grew into incredible young women who love God and serve others.

My high school social studies teacher, Mr. Tom Muench, has made a difference in the lives of countless students over the years. As a teacher, coach, and guidance counselor, he was able to make an impact by taking a personal interest in each student. Because they knew he cared, they respected him and trusted him and listened to him. We still do, to this day. He has thousands of Facebook friends—4,928 at last count—and he remembers and loves and believes in each one. At almost 80 he is still telling jokes, dispensing advice, and encouraging us to be the best people we can be. His Facebook posts reveal his genuine heart. Here is a sampling:

> [Valentine's Day week] Well kids, I prayed for all of us today. I prayed for you and me to try to reach out with the understanding of love. This is the week we think about love. St Paul says, "Love is always patient and kind; love is never jealous; love is not boastful or conceited, it is never rude and never seeks its own advantage, it does not take offence or store up grievances. Love does not rejoice at wrongdoing, but finds its joy in the truth. It is always ready to make allowances, to trust, to hope and to endure whatever comes." (1 Corinthians 13:4-7)

> My prayers are for thanks for a wonderful week and the people that made it that good. Let us all pray or reach out to people who are sick. Pray for the care

givers and the patients. Take some time to visit or call a person in this situation today. Or help a person who has a loved one in this situation.

My prayers tonight are that we try hard to treat people as we would like to be treated. Love the neighbor (neighbor in the largest sense possible), as you love yourself. I also pray forgiveness for not doing this way too often.

Like Peter and the Rowes and Mr. Muench, neither was Paul out to impress anyone with his superior knowledge. He longed for people to know Christ, and he understood that he had to show them how much he cared about them. In his letters he often expressed his love for his readers and assured them that he was praying for them:

> God can testify how I long for all of you with the affection of Christ Jesus (Phil. 1:8).

> Ever since I heard about your faith in the Lord Jesus and your love for all God's people, I have not stopped giving thanks for you, remembering you in my prayers (Eph. 1:15-16).

> Just as a nursing mother cares for her children, so we cared for you. Because we loved you so much, we were delighted to share with you not only the gospel of God but our lives as well (1 Th. 2:7-8).

Paul knew that "knowledge puffs up while love builds up" (1 Cor. 8:1). Even if one "can fathom all mysteries and all knowledge" (1 Cor. 13:2), without love he is nothing. Do Paul's words about love in 1 Corinthians 13 describe the love you have for those you are ministering to? If so, they will be more likely to receive and take to heart the knowledge you impart to them.

---

[1] Community Bible Study Commentary on 1 & 2 Peter, page 112

WHO CHANGES THE HUMAN HEART?

The prophet Jeremiah has a great deal to say about the human heart. In chapter 24 he quotes the words of the Lord:

I will give them a heart to know that I am the LORD, and they shall be my people and I will be their God, for they shall return to me with their whole heart (Jer. 24:7).

It made me wonder, "Does God give them a heart to know that He is the Lord because they have returned to Him with their whole heart? Or do they return to God with their whole heart because He has given them a heart to know that He is the Lord?"

Later in the book Jeremiah makes some similar statements about the heart:

You will seek me and find me, when you seek me with all your heart (Jer. 29:13).

I will give them one heart and one way, that they may fear me forever, for their own good and the good of their children after them (Jer. 32:39).

Do they find God because *they* have sought Him with their whole heart? Or do they fear God because *He* has put it in their heart to do so? Who bears the responsibility? Who takes the credit? Who gets the blame?

There are many more passages that point to both human responsibility and divine sovereignty. The New Testament also speaks of this tension. John says we must receive Christ and believe in His name in order to become children of God, but it is the will of God—*not* the will of man—that brings about the new birth:

> But to all who did receive him, who believed in his name, he gave the right to become children of God, who were born, not of blood nor of the will of the flesh nor of the will of man, but of God (Jn. 1:12-13).

Six verses in John 6 talk about "coming" to Jesus (Jn. 6:35, 37a, 37b, 44, 45, 65). Jesus calls people to take action: to come to Him, believe in Him, and eat the bread of life. He promises that *whoever* comes will be welcomed and blessed; it is an open invitation to everyone. Yet at the same time, He says that the *only* way to come to Him is by being drawn by the Father and given to the Son:

> I am the bread of life; whoever comes to me shall not hunger, and whoever believes in me shall never thirst (Jn. 6:35).

> All that the Father gives me will come to me, and whoever comes to me I will never cast out (Jn. 6:37).

> No one can come to me unless the Father who sent me draws him (Jn. 6:44).

The disciples ask, "What must we do, to be doing the works of God?" (Jn. 6:28). Jesus answers, "This is the work of God, that you believe in him whom he has sent" (6:29). Does He mean that believing in Him is the work *we* must do, or that creating faith in our hearts is the work *He* does in us?

Paul also expresses the interplay between human choice and divine working:

> Therefore, my beloved, as you have always obeyed, so now, not only as in my presence but much more in my absence, work out your own salvation with fear and trembling, for it is God who works in you, both to will and to work for his good pleasure (Phil. 2:12-13).

We see the two principles at work in this passage:

> Work out your own salvation [man's will and work].
> It is God who works in you [God's will and work].

Maybe instead of wrangling about God's sovereignty and man's free will, we should be focusing on working out our own salvation!

"I CAN ONLY IMAGINE"

I can only imagine
What it will be like
When I walk
By your side

I can only imagine
What my eyes will see
When your face
Is before me
I can only imagine.[1]

The death of Bart Millard's father prompted the singer to meditate about heaven and eventually to write the song "I Can Only Imagine," in which he tries to picture what it will be like to be in the presence of Jesus. Sooner or later, particularly after the death of a loved one, most people ponder what life after death will be like. Eric Clapton wrote "Tears in Heaven" after the tragic death of his young son. He asks, "Would you know my name / If I saw you in heaven? / Would you feel the same / If I saw you in heaven?" Johnny Cash asks, "Should you go first or if you follow me / Will you meet me in Heaven some day?" We long to know the answers to questions like these.

Meditating about heaven is good. Contemplating God's awesome works—past, present, and future—causes us to be worshipful and thankful. And thinking about where we are headed changes the way we behave here. Are we looking forward to and preparing for meeting Jesus face to face? Are we living in a way that is pleasing to God, so that we will hear, "Well done, good and faithful servant"? Are we growing in sanctification so that we will be fit to live in His presence for eternity? Our sanctification will not be complete in this life, but the process should be ongoing every day so we are ready for His coming. As Paul said to the Thessalonians, "May God himself, the God of peace, sanctify you through and through. May your whole spirit, soul and body be kept blameless at the coming of our Lord Jesus Christ" (1 Thessalonians 5:23).

So the purpose of this essay is to encourage us to set our hearts and minds on things above, where Christ is seated at the right hand of God (Colossians 3:1). I look at what we know about heaven from Scripture, and I try to draw some reasonable inferences. But much of the essay consists of asking questions and making speculations. My hope is that as we ask the questions and contemplate God's plans and anticipate the fulfillment of His promises, our hearts will feel "a thrill of hope." I believe that as we meditate on the fantastic future that God has in store for us, we will delight in Him even more and want to live now in such a way that we will be ready for His eternal kingdom.

One certainty is that worship will be a central feature of heaven. The most magnificent worship services here on earth are only a pale foretaste of the worship that will take place in heaven. Throughout Revelation (e.g., chapters 4, 5, 7, 11, 15, 19), John describes the outpouring of worship that will continually take place:

> In the center, around the throne, were four living creatures, and they were covered with eyes, in front and in back. The first living creature was like a lion, the second was like an ox, the third had a face like a man, the fourth was like a flying eagle. Each of the four living creatures had six wings and was covered with eyes all around, even under his wings. Day and night they never stop saying:

> "Holy, holy, holy
> is the Lord God Almighty,
> who was, and is, and is to come."
> (4:6-8)

Then I looked and heard the voice of many angels, numbering thousands upon thousands, and ten thousand times ten thousand. They encircled the throne and the living creatures and the elders. In a loud voice they sang:

> Worthy is the Lamb, who was slain,
> to receive power and wealth and wisdom
> and strength and honor and glory and praise!

Then I heard every creature in heaven and on earth and under the earth and on the sea, and all that is in them, singing:

> To him who sits on the throne and to the Lamb
> be praise and honor and glory and power,
> for ever and ever! (5:11-13)

Undoubtedly this worship will be happening continually, but I don't think it's the only thing we will be doing. We know for sure that there will be a spectacular feast—the Wedding Supper of the Lamb (Revelation 19:9). I believe this banquet is more than just a metaphor for the relationship between God and His people, and I don't think it will be the only time we eat in heaven—the trees that bear fruit every month are more than just decoration! Jesus ate and drank in His glorified body, and I believe we will too. At the Last Supper (that is, the last before He died), He suggested that we would eat and drink together in the kingdom of God:

> I have eagerly desired to eat this Passover with you before I suffer. For I tell you, I will not eat it again *until* it finds fulfillment in the kingdom of God.... I will not drink again of the fruit of the vine *until* the kingdom of God comes (Luke 22:15-18).

Here's another thing I have been contemplating with respect to heaven. Before Jesus left earth and ascended into heaven, He promised, "Surely I am with you always, to the very end of the age." As the disciples watched Him leave, they probably wondered how He could possibly be with them if He wasn't even on earth. Now we know that He is with each believer constantly in the person of the Holy Spirit. When we pray, God gives us His undivided attention (infinity divided by anything is still infinity!), as if each person were the only person in the universe. I can only think that in heaven our relationship with God will be even *more* personal and *more* intimate than it is now. I suspect that there will be times when we are alone with the Lord or in a small group, as well as with the whole company of heaven. As Revelation 21:3 says, "Now the dwelling of God is with men, and he will live with them. They will be his people, and God himself will be with them and be their God."

In addition to developing our relationship with God, I also think we will be able to develop our relationships with other people. Better than all the promises of creature comforts, exquisite beauty, and freedom from pain is the anticipation of being with other people in perfect relationships. It is a great joy to look forward to being reunited with those we've lost and meeting those we never knew—the saints who went before us, the father who died before his son was born, babies who died in the womb. The Transfiguration gives us a little glimpse of saints who never knew each other on earth—Moses, Elijah, Peter and company—coming together and talking with Jesus. The disciples were terrified, but Jesus told them to get up and not be afraid (Matthew 17:6–7). At that point it was not the right time to settle down in shelters and have a prolonged visit (because Jesus had not yet accomplished what He came to do), but the time will come!

Besides the healing and growth of personal relationships, the descriptions in Revelation 21 and 22 sound as if there will be healing and peace on a global scale, with nations that were once hostile to God coming to walk in the light:

The city does not need the sun or the moon to shine on it, for the glory of God gives it light, and the Lamb is its lamp. The nations will walk by its light, and the kings of the earth will bring their splendor into it. On no day will its gates ever be shut, for there will be no night there. The glory and honor of the nations will be brought into it (Rev. 21:23-26).

There will be nothing and no one impure in the city—no murderers or adulterers or idolaters or liars. Before they can enter, they have to "wash their robes." *Then* they will "have the right to the tree of life and may go through the gates into the city." They will enjoy the river of the water of life, on either side of which grows the tree of life, whose leaves "are for the healing of the nations."

It will take all of eternity for us to get to know God fully. Besides getting to know Him and getting to know other saints, I think He will also allow us to explore His creation and get to know it. We haven't even begun to fully know our speck of Earth; imagine what else is out there! I think we will be astonished as we see the extent of His extravagant creativity. And will there be books in heaven? Why not? I doubt that we will instantly know everything there is to know; I imagine that we will keep learning and growing forever— whether through experiencing, exploring, reading, talking with other people, or learning directly from God.

Music will definitely have a big role in heaven—voice, harp, trumpet, and probably every other kind of instrument used for worship in the Bible, like tambourine, flute, and lyre. And why not instruments and music styles from every culture? Imagine a heavenly orchestra with every instrument in the world. And unless God Himself or angels or elves make these instruments, somebody will have to do it. I wouldn't be surprised if there were craftsmen creating violins surpassing the Stradivarius and organs more wonderful than those in the greatest cathedrals. And if there will be music in heaven, why not the other arts as well? Dance, drama, painting, sculpture, literature? Jesus is making our homes in heaven, but maybe we'll have architects and carpenters and interior decorators too. Will there be chefs to prepare the wonderful banquets we'll enjoy? How about jewelers for all the precious stones? My husband loves to do math; maybe he'll be able to keep doing it in heaven, discovering more and more about the order in God's universe. What about scientists? Why couldn't there be biologists, astronomers, geologists, chemists, and physicists, to name a few?

I don't presume to know exactly what or when the Millennium will be or how everything will play out in God's plan, but the phase of the Kingdom of God described in passages like Isaiah 11 sounds like a wonderful time of peace and righteousness. In this messianic kingdom, the Branch will bear fruit and the Spirit of the Lord will rest on Him. With righteousness He'll judge the needy, and with justice He'll give decisions for the poor. All the animals will live in harmony (wolf, lamb, leopard, goat, calf, lion, yearling, cow, bear, ox, cobra, viper—and I bet our pets), with a little child leading them. "They will neither harm nor destroy on all my holy mountain, for the earth will be full of the knowledge of the Lord as the waters cover the sea. In that day the Root of Jesse will stand as a banner for the peoples; the nations will rally to him, and his place of rest will be glorious" (vv. 9–10).

Heaven will probably be very different from what any of us think it will be. But it's perfectly fine to imagine the most wonderful place we can conceive of, and then realize that it will be far more so than we can begin to envision. As Paul says, "No eye has seen, no ear has heard, no mind has conceived what God has prepared for those who love him!" (1 Corinthians 2:9).

---

[1] Millard, Bart, "I Can Only Imagine," 1999; recorded by MercyMe

ABOUT THE AUTHOR

Diane Perkins was born in 1953, the eldest of five children, four girls and a boy, born to Phyllis Woolsey Perkins, a registered nurse, and Donald Perkins, an engineer at General Electric in Syracuse, New York. As a girl she was not the domestic type; she preferred sports and adventure to those activities that were considered more appropriate for a girl of that era. Her unladylike behavior included such actions as cutting class to hang out in the music room, flipping pencils up in the air to stick in the styrofoam ceiling so they would later drop on unsuspecting heads, and putting a boy in a headlock on the playground in sixth grade.

By high school she had outgrown the trouble-making and managed to graduate as valedictorian, then headed to Cornell University. During her freshman year, she committed her life to Christ through a campus ministry and also met her future husband, a graduate student in physics named Juan Antonio Castro, playing Ping-Pong at a spiritual retreat. In their naivete as new Christians, they considered the fact that no one could beat them at doubles Ping-Pong as a sign that they were meant to be a team for life.

Tony and Diane spent the first year of their married life in his native Peru and then returned to the States so she could finish her education at a Christian college and he could attend seminary. Their first daughter was born during that time, followed by two more girls and three boys, the girls being born in the Midwest and the boys after the family moved to the North Shore of Massachusetts. She spent the better part of eighteen years as a stay-at-home mom and then the last twenty-five years as a writer and editor of educational materials, while Tony has worked as a college professor, software engineer, and high school physics teacher.

Diane still enjoys hiking, biking, snowboarding, playing volleyball and Ping-Pong, and more recently, doing obstacle races. Most of all, she likes to spend time with her growing family, which now includes eight grandchildren.

Reflections of a Tomboy Grandma represents ten years of intensely examining her faith and writing about what she has learned on her journey from initial delight through a long slog of confusion, uneasiness, and discouragement to a place of deep convictions, genuine joy, and full assurance of God's great purposes for His creation.

Index

A

Abraham, 120–23
Advent, 39
advocate, 73
"All Praise to Thee," by F.
    Bland Tucker, 136
Alvis, Joanna Castro, 145
ambition, 44
Appalachian Trail, 3, 5
arbitrator, 73
Arredondo, Carlos, 113
assurance, 169
Australian floods of 2011, 151
authority, 110
Awakenings, by Oliver Sacks, 58

B

bankruptcy, 42
Barnabas, 24
Bell, George, 3
Bennington, Harry, 14
Bennington, Josh, 14
Big Bang Theory, 115, 118
BioLogos, 117
"Blessings," by Laura Story, 14
Body of Christ, 46
Boston Marathon, 45, 105, 111,
    139
Boston Red Sox, 105
Buell, Jaxon, 4
Bush, Barbara, 163
Bush, George W., 156, 163

C

Calvinism, 131–33
cancer, 14
Capa, Cornell, 50
Cash, Johnny, 217
Castro, Alex, 8, 55, 158
Castro, Andy, 151, 183
Castro, Christine, ii, 105, 113,
    140
Castro, Daniel, 39, 77
Castro, Tony, 79, 121, 151, 157,
    222
Centers for Disease Control and
    Prevention, 157
certainty, 169–73
character of God, 165
childlessness, 124
Chilean mine rescue, 152
Christian Royal Pottery, 4
Christmas, 39
Clapton, Eric, 217
class reunion, 52
Clayton, Fr. Tim, 3
Cocuzzo, Claire Marie, 5
Cohen, Leonard, 105
Collins, Francis, 117
Colvin, Ruth, 156, 161
compassion, 32
complaining, 60
conflict, 24, 166
conflict resolution, 167
conscience, 84